W9-AAA-636

A Primer for Preachers

A Primer
for Preachers

Ian Pitt-Watson

BAKER BOOK HOUSE
Grand Rapids, Michigan 49506

Copyright © 1986 by Baker Books
a division of Baker Book House Company
P.O. Box 6287, Grand Rapids, MI 49516-6287

Library of Congress Catalog Card Number: 86-72370

ISBN: 0-8010-7096-1

Seventh printing, December 1998

Printed in the United States of America

Unless otherwise indicated, Scripture references are from
The New English Bible, copyright 1961, 1970 by the
Delegates of the Oxford University Press and the Syndics
of the Cambridge University Press. Used by permission.
Other translations used are the King James Version (KJV)
and the Revised Standard Version (RSV).

For information about academic books, resources for
Christian leaders, and all new releases available from
Baker Book House, visit our web site:
http://www.bakerbooks.com

With affection and gratitude
to my students, past and present,
at Fuller Theological Seminary

Contents

Introduction

My hope is that this book may serve as a preaching primer for two different constituencies and in two different senses. It is a book designed in the first instance for theological students beginning the study of homiletics. Addressing that constituency it is intended to offer, inevitably from a limited perspective, an introduction to a new subject matter. That is a function that primers are normally expected to fulfill.

But a primer can also be something less didactic and more dynamic, less explanatory and more explosive. A primer can be a small charge used to trigger a much larger detonation. For the theological student it is hoped that this book may fulfill that more exciting function also. The majority of theological students whom I have had the privilege of teaching leave seminary with plenty of theological dynamite in their possession. But, sadly, they seldom look dangerous. Usually the theology is all safely diffused and defused. It is something that someday the student may perhaps explain in the pulpit, but it is hardly something that looks likely to explode there, or anywhere else for that matter. This preaching primer is intended to remind the theological student of the shattering power of the Word of God, of the destructive consequences of its misuse, but above all of the revolutionary potential of that Word to change lives and to change our world. Even the tiniest spark of authentic insight brought by the preacher to the text of Scripture can trigger the irresistible transforming power of God that is both his love and his judgment.

But it is my hope that this preaching primer (in both senses of that word) may be of some service to a second constituency. I am constantly privileged to work with pastors who for many years have faithfully preached, but who know that even the ablest of us need a refresher course from time to time, and that some even of the best of us have grown a little weary in our preaching ministry, lost a little of our youthful sparkle (however brash it may have been), and now fear lest we have lost that vital spark that alone can make *us* "preaching primers" of the Word of God, God's agents in the release of the power, the *dynamis,* the dynamism, the dynamic, the dynamite that we call the Scriptures of the Old and New Testament. For that constituency also, a constituency to which I myself belong, this preaching primer is written.

I owe a debt of gratitude to several of my colleagues and friends on the faculty of Fuller Theological Seminary—especially to Colin Brown, Professor of Systematic Theology, and Donald Hagner, Professor of New Testament, for invaluable guidance in the final stages of the preparation of the manuscript; also to Douglas Nason, Instructor in Preaching, for shrewd advice in selecting the list of books for further reading.

1

What Comes First

The title of this chapter is intended to make a statement, not ask a question. Psychologically, we are all impatient to get on to the "how?" question: how do we preach and how can we do it better? But that is the wrong question to start with. Logically and theologically, "what?" comes first. Anxious seminarians and overworked pastors are hungry for pragmatics. Implicitly or explicitly the teacher of homiletics receives the signal clearly and often: "Tell me how to do it. Don't start by answering theoretical questions that I'm not even asking. The theology can wait, next Sunday's sermon can't."

I too have felt the pressure of that impatience during fifteen impossible, rewarding years as a pastor-preacher. I am also acutely conscious that any communicator who wants to be listened to or read ought to be aware of the risk of ignoring the questions which the listener or reader is first asking and first wants to be answered. But sometimes that risk has to be taken. Right answers are of little use if they are given to the wrong questions. How can I tell you how to do something until first we have agreed what it is that you and I are meant to be doing? The pragmatic "how?" question must indeed be addressed by the homiletician and will be in this book. But the theological "what?" question must come first, however strong the psychological pressures may be to reverse the order.

The reasons for the pressure to ask the wrong questions first are all too obvious. We have come to think of theology as being a purely academic discipline. It can indeed be that, for the academic theologian has his own vital and honorable contribution to make to the life of the church. But a biblical theology can never be merely reflective or academic. It is at heart practical. The New Testament church preached, taught, worshiped, and cared before it did anything else, and certainly before it articulated its reflective theology. The raw materials of practical theology—homiletics, Christian nurture, liturgics, pastoral care—have been there from the beginning, long before systematic theology found a clear voice. We who exercise the functions of a biblical Christian ministry are therefore not merely dependent relatives of our full-time colleagues in reflective theology. We are ourselves practical theologians, no less theologians because we are practical. We not only apply academic theology to the practice of ministry, but also discover it there. Preaching is itself a kind of practical theology. That is why homiletics can never be content to be merely a skills discipline, concerned alone with pragmatics and the question "how?" How *what*?! The answer to the question "what?" must precede the answer to the question "how?" The theology of preaching must determine its methodology and therefore the nature of homiletics itself.

Let me first make clear what homiletics is not. It is not simply a subspecies of speech-communication theory that happens to be about God. If that sounds negative or even arrogantly dismissive, it certainly is not meant to be. Rhetorical theory has a long and honorable history. It was already an integral part of our western culture long before the Christian gospel was first preached, and throughout the Christian centuries the church has treasured and sought enrichment from that ancient classical tradition. It is an aberration of our own century and culture that for most of us the word *rhetoric* carries with it so much negative emotive freight. For men and women of my age who remember World War II, it still irrationally but involuntarily calls to mind the frenetic, satanic eloquence of Adolf Hitler. For younger people, the word tends to suggest, at best, an archaic art form, at worst, an anachronistic pomposity. Mercifully, the work of dedicated and able scholars in the field of rhetorical theory and speech communication has enabled us in recent decades to shed some of our irrational suspicion of the word *rhetoric*. But still if you tell me that what I have said is "pure rhetoric," you are usually not commending my communication skills so much as questioning the sincerity of what I have said. The time is long overdue for the complete reinstatement of rhetoric to an honorable place in our popular vocabulary *and* in our theological curriculum; for interpersonal communication through the spoken word is the lifeblood of Christian community.

But my thesis still stands. Rhetoric and speech communication for the homiletician is not a master discipline of which preaching is a subspecies, the subject matter of which happens to be about God but might equally well be about astrophysics or fishing or George Washington. Precisely because God is the subject of the communication, because preaching *is* about God and not about anything else, it is *sui generis*—in a class by itself. Even to call God the "subject" of the communication or to speak of the communication as being "about" him is to falsify the situation. For in the preaching event it is not just we who are talking "about" God, God being the subject of our talk (or for that matter the object of our inquiry). It is God who is the communicator. It is not just we who are communicating truths about him. He is communicating himself. In his divine foolishness God speaks through our fumblings and bumblings in the pulpit Sunday by Sunday—sometimes because of what we have said, sometimes (I suspect) in spite of it. His Word does not return to him fruitless without accomplishing his purpose (Isa. 55:11).

The Word of God comes to us in three ways: first, in Jesus Christ, the Word made flesh; second, in the written Word of Scripture as contained in the Old and New Testaments; but third (and this is the divine-crazy absurdity), in the Word preached. The Word preached is part of the "foolishness of God" that is wiser than we are (1 Cor. 1:25). The Second Helvetic Confession is outrageously specific: *Praedicatio verbi dei est verbum dei*—the preaching of the Word of God is the Word of God. If this is true, then indeed preaching is a communication transaction like no other. This is not to invalidate the importance of communication theory for the preacher. On the contrary, such a high doctrine of preaching should make us passionately concerned to ensure that we have done everything humanly possible to become the kind of people who in the pulpit will facilitate and not obstruct the Word of God that speaks to us and through us. We preachers need more speech-communication skills, not fewer. That is all too obvious. But these speech-communication skills must be subject to theological scrutiny. They must be seen as a vital part of the discipline of homiletics and thus as a subspecies of practical theology. Homiletics employs communication skills but owes obedience to biblical theology alone. Communication theory is an honored servant of the Word but must never presume to be its master.

The plot thickens. We have said what preaching is not: it is not just a kind of speech communication that happens to be about God. We have said what preaching is or is meant to be: it is God speaking through us who preach. The first answer sounds plausible but negative. The second answer sounds positive but implausible. No wonder anxious seminarians and overworked pastors hunger for pragmatics when even a would-be practical theology of preaching must start by apparently raising more problems than it solves, and by asking more questions than it answers. Yet the questions about the nature of preaching cannot be avoided. Our failure to wrestle honestly with these questions has itself become a major part of the problem. Our uncertainty about what is meant to be happening when we preach has created both in us and in our hearers a profound ambivalence in our attitude towards preaching. The recognition of that ambivalence and the identification of its cause will prove to be a necessary final step in our clearing of the theological ground, and a first step toward a pragmatically relevant answer to the key theological question we are addressing concerning the nature of preaching itself.

Many of us, some consciously and others subconsciously, are disturbed by our own uncertainty about what is supposed to be happening when we preach. Most of us can give an all-purpose formula answer to the question "What is preaching?" Sometimes we point to a text of Scripture or a scriptural model, sometimes we draw on our own traditions and confessions, sometimes our answer to the question is no more than an attempted rationalization and justification of our own practice. But our formulae, even when scripturally based and theologically sound, seldom seem to reflect accurately our own experience and procedures. Homileticians in this regard are especially vulnerable, not least when they are preaching to their own students. Even the most charitable student must find it hard to resist the temptation to "quote the proverb . . . , 'Physician, heal yourself! . . . We have heard of all your doings at Capernaum; do the same here in your own home town'" (Luke 4:23). And, of course, often we cannot. We fail constantly to practice what we preach about preaching—homileticians, preacher-pastors, and student-preachers alike. Hence our ambivalence. Many of us find ourselves torn by conflicting emotions as we mount the pulpit steps. On the one hand we are tense and apprehensive, knowing our own inadequacies for the task ahead. On the other hand, there is an irrepressible part of us that is expectant and exhilarated, knowing that just sometimes things of mysterious power and beauty do happen when we preach, things we could scarcely have imagined, far less created.

Often we preach within the tension of that ambivalence. I have a kind of love-hate relationship with preaching. One part of me would gladly be rid of the stress and burden of it. When I was younger, I thought it would become easier as one became more experienced. I find it is not so, but I no longer wish it to be otherwise. When I stop being scared I think I'll quit, for I suspect that this will mean either that I no longer believe that anything powerful or beautiful can happen, and therefore having nothing to lose I shall have nothing to fear; or else it will mean that I believe myself at last to have obtained a sufficient degree of professional competence to ensure that I will give a good performance. Either way, if ever I lose my fear of preaching and my frustration at my own inadequacies in that task, I suspect it will be a sign that I ought to quit.

Yet, while one part of me would gladly be rid of that burden of fear and frustration, another part of me knows that in the pulpit I find a kind of fulfillment, a joy, an exhilaration like no other. Part of that experience I know can be tarnished and flawed. The pulpit is a great place for an ego trip. But I know there is more to it than that, and that without that "more" I would be painfully impoverished. "It would be misery to me not to preach" (1 Cor. 9:16). I am drawn to that task irresistibly. I love with my whole heart this fearsome, frustrating, burdensome, exhilarating, beautiful thing we face Sunday by Sunday as we mount the pulpit steps. I know I share this strange ambivalence with many others. I see it constantly in the students and pastors I am privileged to teach. I believe it reflects the fact that we often don't know what we are doing when we preach, and we know we ought to know—hence the frustration of it. But I believe it also reflects the fact that God knows precisely what he is doing— hence the exhilaration of it. The recognition of that embarrassing, encouraging paradox may be a first, faltering step toward understanding the impossible claim that "the preaching of the Word of God is the Word of God."

But that ambivalence towards preaching in many of us who are preachers is not ours alone. It is shared by many of those to whom we preach. They too have a love-hate relationship with it. The love is there and is real. We are seeing in many of our churches a hunger for preaching and a genuine love of the Word, not least among the young, that offers rich promise for the years ahead. Across the whole face of Christendom Christians have been rediscovering the Bible. That is the root of the resurgence of interest in preaching that we have been witnessing, and it may well be a sign, as it was at the time of the Reformation, that a new reformation is already upon us. We must hope and pray that this is so, and that this time we may be guided by God to gather the rich harvest of his Word without sowing the bitter seeds of sectarianism. But whatever the future may hold in that regard, the present is full of promise for the preacher. I doubt if ever the ability to preach has stood higher in the list of priorities of the average pastor search committee. Indeed it may well be that in some quarters the pendulum has swung too far and that other functions of ministry, pastoral and liturgical, have been undervalued as preaching has been exalted. However that may be, there is little doubt that ordinary people in our churches are saying loudly and clearly, "Give us more and better preaching." The love is there.

But, as with us so with our hearers, that attraction to preaching is part of a love-hate relationship. For our hearers the hate element is partly an inevitable consequence of their disappointment and disillusionment when our ineptitude in the pulpit so often falls short of their expectations. But precisely what they expect is usually very ill-defined. That is the root cause of their ambivalence about preaching, as it is the root cause of ours. They don't quite know what to expect, just as we don't know what is expected of us. So preacher and congregation make a few pragmatic adjustments until some compromised role expectation for the preacher has been tacitly agreed on. Sadly, the result is sometimes an endless series of sermons on the same theme:

"It's nice to be nice and it's good to be good, and if we're nice, good people Jesus will help us to become even nicer and better." No one is really satisfied with this as a preaching model, but no one is actually offended, so it stays.

Below the surface, however, tension is mounting in the listener, and sooner or later the frustration must find voice. When it comes it is usually a scream of protest that no one ever hears, but that the preacher can read all too easily in the body language of the congregation. The flaccid postures and dead faces cry to heaven with one voice: "Stop preaching at me!" What has happened? It is worth noting what usually has happened when in ordinary conversation we say to one another, "Stop preaching!" It is invariably meant to be a severe rebuke. I say it to someone who is making me angry by insisting on telling me what to do and what not to do. I am not angry because the moral precepts being offered me are untrue—if that were the case I would say, "Stop talking nonsense." I am angry because I am being told what I already know to be true and suspect to be no less true of the one who is "preaching at me." I already know that I am not what I ought to be; I know I am doing things that I ought not to do and that I am leaving undone things I ought to do. Like most people, I do not live my life crippled by moral indecision, paralyzed for lack of good advice. For the most part, I know what to do; I'm just not very good at doing it. My problem is not my moral indecision, but my moral impotence.

Paul describes that human predicament with precision and passion.

When I want to do the right, only the wrong is within my reach. In my inmost self I delight in the law of God, but I perceive that there is in my bodily members a different law, fighting against the law that my reason approves and making me a prisoner under the law that is in my members, the law of sin. Miserable creature that I am, who is there to rescue me out of this body doomed to death? God alone, through Jesus Christ our Lord! Thanks be to God! [Rom. 7:21–25]

Notice how Paul's ethical analysis of our human predicament (including his own) flows not into moral prescription and exhortation, but into a kind of doxology. Why? Because "what the law could never do, because our lower nature robbed it of all potency, God has done: by sending his own Son . . ." (Rom. 8:3). Paul knows that the problem is not our indecision but our impotence, and that the remedy will not be good advice about what we ought to do, but good news about what God has done. "Don't preach!" Paul was used to hearing that rebuke from people who thought he was playing with antinomian fire and talking dangerous nonsense. But neither friend nor foe ever accused Paul of preaching a vain repetition of boring moral platitudes—"It's nice to be nice and it's good to be good, for Jesus' sake, amen." I wish the same were true of us when overtly or covertly we receive the rebuke, "Don't preach!" But broken eye contact between us and the congregation, their body language, and the discreet rustle of candy papers sometimes sadly suggest another conclusion.

Now at last we are in a position to attempt a direct answer to the question with which we began. What is preaching? We have seen already that if, in some divine-crazy way, *God* is the communicator in the preaching event (1 Cor. 1:21), then preaching is not just a special kind of human speech communication that happens to be about God. The implausible conclusion of the Second Helvetic Confession becomes inescapable: "The preaching of the Word of God is the Word of God." We have seen also how the ambivalence of our experience as preachers seems to affirm both the truth and the implausibility of that high doctrine of preaching. But it is the ambivalence of our hearers that takes us to the heart of the matter. The hunger for preaching is not a hunger for *any* kind of religious or moral talk. It is a hunger for the hearing of the Word of God. That hunger is not being satisfied because often what we are saying in our pulpits is not firmly rooted in God's written Word, our sole and sufficient authority for saying anything. If people, hungry for bread, are offered a stone, we need not be surprised if our preaching receives a stony response.

But this is not merely to indict the kind of blatantly unbiblical preaching that clearly uses texts (if at all) as mere pretexts. Those of us who, like myself, are wholeheartedly and unambiguously committed to the authority of Scripture as our supreme rule of faith and life do well to remember that the frequency with which we quote Scripture in our preaching is no reliable index of the biblical authenticity of what we are saying. Satan too can quote Scripture (Matt. 4:6)! Indeed, there is no doctrine, however heretical, and no action, however immoral, that cannot be proof-texted from Scripture with the assistance of a large enough concordance and just a little perverted ingenuity. It is not lack of sufficient biblical quotation that usually occasions the silent protest from the pews (slumped bodies and dull, downcast eyes) that says so clearly, "Stop preaching!" The heart of the dis-ease lies elsewhere.

We have debased the word *preaching;* we have distorted the authentic *biblical* nature of the event; we have forgotten what the word means. As I said at the outset, we have been so anxious to ask the "How do you do it?" question that we have forgotten to ask the prior "What are we meant to be doing?" question. I remember as a small boy thinking that "How do you do?" was a silly question to ask when people met one another. I often wanted to reply, "How do you do what?" (For years I was convinced that Tweedledum or Tweedledee, those famous experts in semantics, had asked that question of Alice in Wonderland. They should have, but they didn't.) In later years I have found myself constantly confronted with "How do you dos?" from students of homiletics, and have at last found the nerve to indulge my childhood fantasy by responding, "How do you do what?" "What?" comes first.

What is preaching? It is proclamation, not just moralizing. It is Good News, not just good advice; it is gospel, not just law. Supremely, it is about God and what he has done, not just about us and about what we ought to do. Logically and theologically (though by no means always chronologically) preaching is about God before it is about us; it is about what God has done before it is about what we ought to do. Our self-understanding must flow from our understanding of God. When we speak of what we ought to do (as of course we must) our moral imperatives must issue from our knowledge of what God has done. Otherwise our imperatives are no more than pious moralizings that refuse to face the facts of life: "When I want to do the right, only the wrong is within my reach" (Rom. 7:21). Or else, if the moral exhortations are seriously intended and seriously attempted, the consequence is simply to compound in our hearers their burden of guilt when, inevitably, they make the same desolating discovery that Paul made: "The good which I want to do, I fail to do; but what I do is the wrong which is against my will" (Rom. 7:19). Only through what God is and has done can I be what I ought to be and do what I ought to do. What I cannot do for myself, "what the law could never do, because [my] lower nature robbed it of all potency, *God has done.*" At heart, preaching is about what "God has done: by sending his own Son in a form like that of our own sinful nature" (Rom. 8:3). That is the gospel.

The practical consequences of these theological conclusions are of immense importance to the preacher. Now that the "what?" question has been faced, the "how do you dos" of preaching can be answered with more confidence. If preaching is to be proclamation and not mere moralizing, then the ethics of our preaching must be rooted in the theology of our preaching. We cannot make sense of who we are and what we ought to do until first we know who God is and what he has done in Jesus Christ. The Christian ethic, severed from its theological roots, is no more than a new law, more demanding and therefore more burdensome than the old. That is why it is always so clear in the letters of Paul that the ethic flows out of the theology. We can be what we ought to be and do what we ought to do only because of what God is and has done. The theology empowers the ethic; it does not just accompany it with an encouraging, heavenly-father pat on the back. For every imperative of the Christian ethic there is an empowering indicative of Christian theology. In the Sermon on the Mount the imperatives are indeed there and inescapable in their demand. But they are more than imperatives; they are descriptions of life in the kingdom of God, indicatives of that kingdom. Perhaps that is why the Sermon begins, not in the imperative mood speaking of how things ought to be, but in the indicative mood speaking of how things are. "How blest are those who know their need of God; the kingdom of heaven is theirs" (Matt. 5:3). This is how things are in the kingdom that in Christ is already in our midst. People are happy *(makarios)* with the special kind of happiness that comes from God alone. The most surprising people are happy in the most surprising circumstances. They are not told to be happy or trying to be happy. They just are happy. The blessed indicative of the Beatitudes precedes and empowers the demanding imperatives of the kingdom that are to follow.

"Don't preach!" means "Don't just tell me what to do; help me to do it." That is precisely what authentic biblical preaching is all about. It is about action enabled by insight, imperatives empowered by indicatives, ethics rooted in theology, "what we ought to do" made possible by what God has done.

2

Two Stories, His and Ours

We have recognized that in preaching, as in other things, the question "what?" must precede the question "how?" and we have attempted at least a provisional answer to the question "What is preaching?" In consequence we can now respond more cordially and with greater confidence to the "How do you dos?" of homiletic enquirers. The "how?" question is now appropriate and meaningful. How do you preach? The simple answer is, we must preach biblically or not at all. If what I am saying is not rooted in Scripture, then, however interesting or edifying it may be, it is not preaching. Preaching is *kerygma*, the proclamation of what God has done in Jesus Christ. The sole source of our knowledge of what God has done comes to us through the text of Scripture under the guidance of the Holy Spirit. We neither have nor require any other authority.

In one sense, therefore, all authentic preaching is expository preaching because it derives its substance from Scripture and is an "exposition" of it. When the word is used in this sense, biblical preaching and expository preaching are synonymous. But sometimes the word is employed in a more limited sense to describe not the substance but the form of

23

the sermon, not its theology, but its methodology. "Expository" as descriptive of a sermon's methodology often means that the preacher works systematically, verse by verse, section by section, through a passage of Scripture, a procedure that can yield a whole series of sermons, sometimes covering a whole book. This expository methodology can be rich and satisfying. It certainly formed a significant part of my own teaching ministry as a pastor-preacher. But I was always aware that the expository methodology I was employing was no guarantee that what I was saying was authentically biblical. Sometimes, on a bad day, it could turn out to be no more than saying weakly, inaccurately, and at length what the Bible was saying for itself with power, precision, and economy. Even on a relatively good day I would sometimes find that I had said a lot about a little, but not much about anything. This is in no way to denigrate the value and potential power of working one's way systematically through the text; it is simply to stress that no methodology can guarantee that a sermon is really biblical. That will be determined not by the sermon's form, but by its content.

To be biblical a sermon must be rooted in the particularities of a passage of Scripture, in the immediate and wider context of the passage and in the cosmic sweep of the Christian gospel as a whole. Only thus can I be sure that I have heard an authentic proclamation of the Word—not just that I have admired the silver-tongued eloquence of the King's herald or even the splendor of his robes, but that I have caught a fresh glimpse of the face of the King himself. The preacher cannot guarantee that this will happen. The preaching event, that moment of royal meeting, is something we cannot create or command. Only God can do that. We can only facilitate it or obstruct its happening. The task of homiletics is to ensure that we more often facilitate and less often obstruct what God is doing through us in the preaching event.

The preaching event is facilitated when we recognize not

just what God has revealed to us, but how he has revealed it; and I believe we can identify an overarching communications strategy, the "binding" of the whole Bible, the thing that holds it all together and makes it for us not many books but one. In identifying that strategy and in understanding its purpose we shall find that our shared recognition of that purpose will prove far more important than the diversity of our homiletic procedures. The gospel we preach has come to us through the Scriptures of Old and New Testaments in the telling of two stories, the Christ story and our stories. If we are to think biblically about the Bible and about the revelation of God in Christ which it contains we must constantly remind ourselves that God has chosen to reveal himself not in terms of philosophical abstractions and concepts, but in terms of these two stories, his and ours. The stories are not merely illustrations of the revelation of God in Christ; they are that revelation. The Christian faith is rooted in history (which for us means ultimately his story), not in some ideal world of eternal truths. The truth is the Event and the Event is what God has done in our creation and our re-creation, in what he is doing now and in what he yet will do before the story ends. At the heart of it, preaching is the telling and retelling of Christ's story and our stories from creation to parousia. It is the *remembering* of the stories with the special kind of remembrance of which the Bible speaks (Old Testament *zakar*, New Testament *anamnesis*), a remembrance that does not merely call to mind the thing remembered, but that makes it real, present, potent, and demanding here and now.

Every preacher knows the power of a good story. But often we think of the story as being at best an illustration of something more important than the story itself, at worst as being the sugar-coating on the bitter pill of the conceptual truth we hope to persuade our hearers to swallow. We have just seen, however, that the Christian gospel does not come to us in Scripture as a "theology"—as a set of conceptual truths about God. The gospel comes to us as story, his story in our stories, and ours in his. The conceptual truths about God which the Bible contains are the fruit of reflection on the story of what God has done, is doing, and will do. The Bible offers no systematic theology. The task of systematizing is the responsibility of the reflective theologian. But the gospel itself comes to us in Scripture not as a system of ideas, but as a series of stories, separate episodes, yet all part of the same story—the continuing story of God's purpose for his people.

This means that, for the preacher, storytelling is more than a way of illustrating the truths of the Christian faith, for these truths have come to us in story form. The story is not less than the true things we can say about it. It is more. Notice that in talking like this about storying we are not simply drawing homiletic conclusions from the obvious truth known to every communicator, that a story is a good way of "getting across" what one wants to say to an audience. We are drawing conclusions from what is obviously true of Scripture itself. The telling of the story of the saving acts of God in Christ from creation to parousia is God's chosen way of getting himself across to us. As we tell and retell the Christ story we share in God's own strategy of communication.

Let us look at the story. Where and when does it begin? It begins "in the beginning."

> When all things began, the Word already was. The Word dwelt with God, and what God was, the Word was. The Word, then, was with God at the beginning, and through him all things came to be; no single thing was created without him. All that came to be was alive with his life, and that life was the light of men. The light shines on in the dark, and the darkness has never mastered it. [John 1:1–5]

This is the theological dynamite that we have so often defused and diffused in our preaching so that we have almost lost sight of the sublime, saving absurdity of it. John is talking about Jesus Christ, about a crucified carpenter. No sooner do we raise the curtain on the Christ story than it sweeps us off our feet with the Pentecostal power of its wild, ecstatic claim that a crucified carpenter with nail-pierced hands made the universe! Paul celebrates the same divine-crazy sublimity when he describes Christ crucified as

the image of the invisible God; his is the primacy over all created things. In him everything in heaven and on earth was created, not only things visible but also the invisible orders of thrones, sovereignties, authorities, and powers: the whole universe has been created through him and for him. And he exists before everything, and all things are held together in him. [Col. 1:15–17]

The author of the letter to the Hebrews begins with the same fanfare of trumpets for the Lord of the universe.

When in former times God spoke to our forefathers, he spoke in fragmentary and varied fashion through the prophets. But in this the final age he has spoken to us in the Son whom he has made heir to the whole universe, and through whom he created all orders of existence: the Son who is the effulgence of God's splendour and the stamp of God's very being, and sustains the universe by his word of power. [Heb. 1:1–3]

This is the beginning of the Christ story, and it is dynamite. Sunday by Sunday we carry this stuff into the pulpit with casual familiarity, never dreaming that even a tiny spark from us could prime a detonation of the Word of God that ought to rock our church to its foundations, maybe even destroy it and rebuild it in three days (John 2:19)! We must preach the Logos, his story, beginning "in the beginning." Much of our preaching is eviscerated because we tell the Christ story as if it began in a Bethlehem stable and ended on the day of the ascension. When all things began he already was. His story is a story of a crucified carpenter whose death and resurrection long ago and far away give meaning and purpose not only to our individual lives, but also to the whole created universe. "The whole universe has been created through him and for him" (Col. 1:16). If that is true, then there is nothing in all creation, nothing in human experience of joy or pain, nothing in the physical world from the galaxies to the atom that cannot be a theophany, a Christophany, a revelation of God in Christ. Paul says it with matchless power:

> I am convinced that there is nothing in death or life, in the realm of spirits or superhuman powers, in the world as it is or the world as it shall be, in the forces of the universe, in heights or depths—nothing in all creation that can separate us from the love of God in Christ Jesus our Lord. [Rom. 8:38–39]

That is not just a mighty word of reassurance to hurting yet triumphant Christians in ancient Rome. It is a statement of how things are. There is no place or time or circumstance where the love of God in Christ is not to be found. We must preach that in the particularities of *our* place and time and circumstance, for how else shall *we* be "convinced"? But we must preach it also in the cosmic sweep of Paul's certainty that Christ, who was and is and is to come, embraces not just our individual personal pieties, but the whole created universe with his arms outstretched on a cross.

The Christ story begins in the beginning; and so do our stories. Our stories did not begin on the day we were born, for our stories are part of the larger story, the Adam story. "God created man (Hebrew *Adam*) in his own image; in the image of God he created him; male and female he created them" (Gen. 1:27). That is when our stories began, not just on the day of our birth, but "in the beginning." Our stories are a part of the story of Adam and Eve and Mr. and Mrs. Adamson and all the kids. If we forget that, we can become trapped in an individualism that is profoundly unbiblical. An inadequate Christian anthropology can be almost as dangerous to preaching as an inadequate Christology. "God saw all that he had made, and it was very good" (Gen. 1:31).

And that included Adam and Eve. Sometimes we are in such a hurry to get on to Genesis 3 that we forget that the Adam story begins not in shame but in glory. When God made Adam male and female in his own image God made humankind glorious and for glory. Then something happened. We do not know the what or the when of it, but we know that something happened that soiled and spoiled the original goodness of God's creation. The magnitude of the calamity that is storied in Genesis 3 can be fully appreciated only by those who have begun the story at the beginning in Genesis 1 and have celebrated the splendors of God's good creation.

Christian orthodoxy has often failed sufficiently to celebrate the original goodness of Genesis 1, and in consequence has been in danger of inducing in orthodox preaching not just appropriate guilt feelings (guilt feelings are appropriate if you are guilty), but unhealthy feelings of self-hatred. The measure of that failure of evangelical orthodoxy may be gauged by the success of some preaching ministries which have done exactly the opposite. They have majored on the theme of self-esteem and muted all reference to sin and guilt. This kind of preaching seems to me to be dangerously unbiblical. Our response to it, however, should not be simply to throw up our hands in horror, but rather to learn from it that we must look again at the Adam story and remember when we preach it to begin "in the beginning." We hear so many sermons on the theme "What went wrong?" That is a good title for a sermon on Genesis 3, and we need to hear such sermons. But we could do with more sermons on the theme "What went right?" The answer to that question throbs like a refrain through Genesis 1: "God said . . . and it was . . . and it was good."

The "how?" of preaching begins in the telling and retelling of God's story and our stories. Both begin in the beginning. The failure to tell adequately *the beginning* of the stories often results in preaching that is inadequate both in its Christology and in its Christian anthropology. We be-

come unbiblical and partial in our understanding both of
Christ and of ourselves because in both cases we have forgotten to begin "in the beginning."

Now let us see how the story goes on. It is a story of God's
purpose for his people; the story of Abraham and Isaac and
Jacob; the story of his chosen people Israel; the story of bond-
age in Egypt, liberation, wilderness wanderings, and the
finding of a Promised Land; the story of covenant and apostasy, of exile in Babylon, of return to Jerusalem, of blessing
and judgment. And in it all and through it all is the story of
a restless prophetic longing for the day when Messiah would
come to vindicate his people and make God's purpose clear.
All this is from the Old Testament, but all this is part of the
Christ story, for he was there in the beginning as surely as
was "the Spirit of God [that] moved upon the face of the wa-
ters" (Gen. 1:2, KJV). I preach constantly from the Old Testament. I try very hard to let the Old Testament passage
speak for itself. I certainly never drag Christ into it, but I
find it almost impossible to keep him out of it. This used to
worry me, as I know such preaching still worries some of my
academic colleagues who are Old Testament scholars. Now I
am unrepentant. If I really believe that Christ was there in
the beginning with the Father and the Holy Spirit, one God,
by whom all things were made and are being remade, then
there is no place, time, or circumstance in which I may not
expect to meet Christ—certainly no place in God's holy
Word. So I believe we must preach the Old Testament,
not just as a curtain raiser to the story that begins in
Bethlehem, but as a part of the Christ story that begins in
the beginning.

The story, of course, climaxes in the birth of the baby, the
life of the person that that baby became, in the things he
taught and did; supremely the story climaxes in the way he
died and in what happened after he died, in his resurrection
and ascension, in the fulfillment of his promise at Pentecost
and the sure hope that the story will not end until he has
come again with power.

We have already seen that from the beginning our story has been mixed up with his. As the two stories unfold they become even more closely enmeshed. The Bible has this strange Pentecostal power that as we read its stories we become a part of the story.

> When Israel was in Egypt land,
>   Let my people go,
> Oppressed so hard they could not stand,
>   Let my people go.
> Go down, Moses, 'way down in Egypt land,
>   Tell old Pharaoh to let my people go.

What did these words mean to the black slaves who first sang them? They were of course speaking about something that had happened long ago and far away. But these words meant more than that. The thing remembered had become a part of their lives, and their lives a part of the thing remembered.

> Were you there when they crucified my Lord?
>   O sometimes it causes me to tremble, tremble, tremble.
> Were you there when they crucified my Lord?

What do these words mean for us? The literal answer is "No, we were not there; 'they' crucified the Lord." But the answer expected by the rhetorical question is clearly yes, and that answer is echoed in our hearts. That is what causes *us* to tremble. The thing remembered that happened long ago and far away has become a part of our lives, and our lives a part of the thing remembered. We were there!

Often our preaching is unbiblical and fails because when we remember the story of what God has done our remembrance is no more than a calling to mind of something that is past and gone. But we have already noticed that when the Bible speaks of remembering it means far more than that. It speaks of a concrete remembrance. The verb *zakar* in the Old Testament is usually used with God as its subject.

When God remembers his people, he does not just give them a kind thought; he blesses them in quite specific and concrete ways. That biblical usage is still lodged in modern English usage when, for instance, we say we have "remembered someone in our will." A kind thought in a codicil would hardly seem adequate. In the same way, small children at a party fully understand the meaning of *zakar* when the candies are passed around and an urgent chorus of voices responds, "Remember me." When Jesus in the upper room said, "Remember me," he meant much more than "Don't forget me." How could they ever forget him? They knew the remembrance of which he spoke made the thing remembered no mere calling to mind of something past and gone. He spoke of a demanding and costly remembrance. (It cost Christ the cross so to remember us in forgiveness and in blessing.) If our remembrance of him is to be real in the sacrament of the Lord's Supper *or in preaching,* it too must cost something in repentance and gratitude. That is part of what "causes me to tremble" every time I remember the story of what he has done.

In that telling and retelling of "the old, old story" as contained in the Scriptures of the Old and New Testaments, the preaching event is born. As we tell it, our story is drawn into his. As we tell our stories of slavery, liberation, wilderness wanderings, crossing Jordan, covenant, apostasy, exile, restoration, dispersion, we find that the story we are telling has become a part of his story, caught up in its demands and blessings. But, supremely, we find our stories caught up in his as we tell of the birth, life, death, resurrection, and reign of Jesus Christ. As we remember that story of how God in Christ has remembered us, our stories become a part of his, and we begin to live "in Christ." Now the gospel is no longer the story of something that God did once for all, far away, there and then. It is now also the story of our world, our societies, our churches, our individual lives in all the infinite complexity and strange amalgam of glory and shame that they present. God did not close up shop on the day of Pentecost. Christ is not sitting at the right hand of God the Father like an actor quietly resting till someone tells him he is due back on the stage for his second coming. Christ is alive and awake, our great High Priest and Advocate, active and potent here and now. However theologically sound, however exegetically accurate, however historically informative, however interesting or inspiring, until the once for all, there and then, saving acts of God in Christ have become embedded in *our* experience, *our* culture, *our* history, *our* individual lives, we have not preached. For preaching is not just the remembering of his story; it is also the remembering of ours.

Above all, preaching is the remembering and retelling of how our stories are being gathered into his. The two stories become one as we begin to live, however imperfectly, "in Christ"; as we begin to get the feel of what Paul is talking about when he says, "the life I now live is not my life, but the life which Christ lives in me" (Gal. 2:20). We are to preach the Good News that in Christ a new kind of life has been made possible here and now, a new kind of humanity has been born, Christ himself the first fruits of that new creation (1 Cor. 15:23). The critical battle with the power of darkness has been fought and won, not by us, but by Christ. The war is not yet over, but the outcome is no longer in doubt. The king of creation, who once rode into town on a donkey to be crowned with thorns and enthroned on a cross, will come again with power to claim his kingdom.

When and how it will be we do not know. "It is not for you to know," Christ said (Acts 1:7). But we do know that that is how the story will end, and what little we know we must preach. We must preach about death and life after death, about heaven and hell, about the second coming of Christ and the final judgment. The tendency is for preachers, depending on their tradition, either to speak of these things as little as possible or else to speak of almost nothing else. For most in my tradition I suspect the danger is to say too little, not too much. However that may be, any preaching that claims to be biblical but that ignores these eschatological themes is self-deceived and deceptive. The New Testament cannot be preached honestly in its integrity by anyone who is prepared to leave these matters to "hell-fire preachers" or sectarian extremists. The two stories we tell, the Christ story and our stories, are not finished yet, and we must speak with modesty and reticence of a future that belongs to God alone. But we cannot be silent. The stakes are too high. In our preaching we must tell and retell the two stories, Christ's and ours, as far as we know them for certain; and today is as far as we know for certain. The future is uncertain, but it is not unknown for those who know Christ. And we know for certain how his story will end. Preach it, preachers!

3

The Text of Scripture

The heart of preaching is the telling of two stories, his story and our stories. The stories are revealed to us in two texts. The normative text, our primary authority for all we say in preaching, is the text of Scripture which tells the Christ story and the Adam story. But preaching which is rooted in the text of Scripture alone can still be unbiblical, unreal, and irrelevant unless it is also rooted in the text of life. By the text of life I mean simply the flow of events and influences that together constitute life as we live it in our world, in our culture, in our society, in our churches, in our homes, and in our hearts. Preaching concerns the Christ who is alive and at work in our world and, knowing what he has already done as revealed in the text of Scripture, we can identify what he is doing now as revealed in the text of life.

Both texts require of the preacher reverent, rigorous exegesis. The exegesis of the text of Scripture is a familiar discipline to any theological student, and in this chapter we shall be looking at some of the ways in which exegetical procedures relate to the preaching task. In the next chapter we shall be concerned with another kind of exegesis which is the special province of the homiletician. We

shall call it "exegesis of life." The text of life, as we read it
in the lives we live and the world about us, requires the
same theological scrutiny that the exegete brings to the text
of Scripture; for the same God, revealed in Christ through
the Holy Spirit in the text of Scripture, is revealing himself
to us now in the text of life.

Let us first look at the relationship between the exegetical procedures we learn as theological students and the task
we face Sunday by Sunday as we mount the pulpit steps. For
any student preparing for Christian ministry, biblical studies are not just a continuation of his liberal-arts education.
Exegetical skills are taught in seminary because of their vo-
cational relevance and because they are meant to be used,
especially in the pulpit. Before I can preach with confidence
on any passage, I must ask of it certain questions (though I
know that not all of these questions will find assured answers). Who wrote this, when, where, why, and for whom?
What did these words mean to those who first read them
in the particularities of their time and culture, and what
do they mean to us in the particularities of ours? How accurately do the manuscripts that have come down to us
through the centuries reflect the original manuscripts
which for us, though lost, are normative? What is the immediate context of these words, the wider context as they relate
to the book from which they are taken, and their still wider
context within the biblical revelation as a whole? These and
many other exegetical and theological questions are all relevant to the preacher, and we must be prepared to ask all or
any of them. But we cannot expect that there will be clear
answers to all the questions, and we certainly ought not to
feel ourselves obliged always to be burdening our listeners
with questions they are not asking and answers we have
not found.

Most of the exegetical work that goes into the preparation
of the sermon will never break surface in the pulpit. It will
be like that greater part of an iceberg that never sees the
light but that keeps the rest afloat. Much of this submerged

exegesis will be material drawn from commentaries on the passage to be preached. It may or may not be interesting to the preacher. But even if it is interesting, unless it is relevant to the central thrust of the sermon, the interest may prove to be merely academic. If so it will probably also be digressive, and in consequence will be better omitted or left implicit. One sometimes witnesses the attempt to establish the biblical credentials of a sermon by offering a digest of all the commentaries the preacher has read (including the use of as many Hebrew and Greek words as possible). That kind of justification by vicarious scholarship seldom works and is theologically no more responsible than the attempt to claim biblical credentials solely through a proliferation of proof-texting.

All preachers will find their own appropriate exegetical procedures. I find I am best helped by first reading and re-reading, thoughtfully and prayerfully, the passage on which I am going to preach. (I have to confess that when I was in Scotland and was trying to pastor a congregation of nearly three thousand people while preaching and teaching three times a week, I lost my earlier discipline in the regular use of the Hebrew and Greek texts. My own academic interests and skills have always been theological rather than linguistic. This is not an excuse, simply a confession.) Next, I read the passage in several reliable translations. It is important for me to discover what the passage is saying to me in my own tongue (Acts 2:6). Only then, thirdly, do I turn to my commentaries and to my Hebrew and Greek texts. I look not only at the verse-by-verse commentary on the passage, but also at the introduction with which the whole commentary begins, thus setting the text in its wider context. Many of the most helpful insights that biblical scholarship has to offer the preacher are overlooked because this introductory material, being relevant to the book as a whole, may not be found in the detailed exegesis of any particular passage. Fourthly, I note any individual words in the passage that I recognize to be theologically loaded and check them out in a

modest-sized theological wordbook (the multivolumed wordbooks are magnificent but too detailed for this purpose and
at this stage, at least for most busy pastor-preachers).
Fifthly, in the light of this economical but rigorous exami-
nation of the text, I will write a free paraphrase in my own
words identifying what the passage is saying. Sixthly, from
that paraphrase I will try to distill a single sentence that
contains the essence of the sermon I am going to preach. I
spend a lot of time on that theme sentence. It should be a
simple sentence with no relative clauses and no big words.
(Until we can say what we have to say in Anglo-Saxon, lay-
ing aside our polysyllabic, seminary-induced Latin- and
Greek-rooted vocabulary we probably do not know what we
are talking about.) Finally, I will write another single sentence, this time not a theme sentence, but a purpose statement answering the questions "Why am I talking about
this passage and what do I expect this sermon to achieve?"
My purpose need not be identical with the original purpose
of the author, but it must be consonant with it. Only honest
exegesis can adjudicate whether it is so or not.

If some of this sounds a little mechanical and even negative, it is certainly not meant to be so, and does not prove to
be so in practice. I deplore the tendency among some students to approach their exegetical task defensively. They already know what they are going to say and are turning to
their commentaries just to be sure that they are not going to
commit any blatant exegetical blooper. All of us know the
frustration of finding that some commentary has just shot a
hole in the head of what we had thought was one of our better sermons. But, in spite of that, we preachers must see the
exegete as our ally, not our enemy. Often we will find if we
look honestly at our own preaching that the best of it is the
fruit of exegetical insights and procedures we have learned
as students that have now become an integral part of our
own way of thinking. On other occasions we will find that
our own partial insights into the passage, though not repu-
diated, are greatly enriched by what the exegete has to

teach us. On yet other occasions we do find that our own first
instincts were just plain wrong, and we can thank God that
the exegete is there to put us right. Let me give some specific
examples of some of the ways in which the exegete, if we will
allow him, can act as our trusted and effective ally.

First, let us see how the recognition of the relevance of
exegetical insights *we already possess* can bring a passage
to life in a way that pulls us into the world of the Bible and
identifies that world in ours. Suppose we are preparing a
sermon for Palm Sunday (Matt. 21:1–11; Mark 11:1–11;
Luke 19:28–40). We have been conditioned to major on the
palm branches and the children shouting, "Three cheers for
Jesus!" minoring on other things that we all know to be a
part of the story. For instance:

> It was a moment of great danger that at any time could
> erupt into violence. It was the Passover season, Indepen-
> dence Day, July fourth, the season that celebrated the liber-
> ation of Israel from bondage in Egypt. But now Israel was
> again in bondage, an occupied country under the heel of
> Rome. Independence Day in the capital of an occupied coun-
> try was always a dangerous time—not least if that capital
> was Jerusalem. Jews not just from Palestine but from all
> over the world converged every year on the city, more than
> two million of them, drawn together by a dangerous amal-
> gam of religion and politics, their shared love for Yahweh
> and their shared hatred of Rome. Every year Passover was
> a dangerous time, but never more dangerous than this year
> with the young Galilean about to ride into town like some
> would-be Messiah. The city was a powder keg ready to ex-
> plode. Everyone knew that. Pilate knew it—the security
> forces kept a low profile but were there in strength.
> Caiaphas knew it and was playing his cards very carefully.
> The Zealots knew it, freedom fighters, urban guerillas or
> terrorists, depending on your politics, lacking only leader-
> ship to enable them to give the Roman garrison a Passover
> they wouldn't soon forget. The disciples knew it—Peter had
> been right at Caesarea Philippi, they should never have
> come. Jesus knew it—knew that in a few days he would be

surrounded by another crowd (or was it the same people?)
shouting not "Hosanna!" but "Crucify!" But still he rode
on, on that miserable donkey that meant he came in peace.
Couldn't he even afford a horse to show that he meant business this time? Then at least the Zealots could have made a
fight of it . . .

That short, summarized passage from a Palm Sunday
sermon certainly contains no fresh or profound exegetical
insights. All of us know the Passover setting of the trium-
phal entry, and know what Passover meant and means to
any devout Jew. All of us know the religious and political
crosscurrents that sweep through the Passion narrative and
that are represented by Pilate, Caiaphas, the Zealots, and
the rest. All of us know (I think) about the donkey and the
horse—the one signifying peace, the other war. The important thing is to be able to remember what we already know
at the right time. With most students I find my task is not to
give them exegetical information they do not already possess (that is done with far greater competence and authority
than I could ever command by colleagues who teach Old and
New Testament studies). My task is to help students see the
relevance of what they do already know, and then to communicate what they know not just as conceptual information,
but as part of the preaching event—as part of his story in
ours. In the example just given, what we know about a variety of things, from Passover to donkeys, becomes part of the
Palm Sunday story.

But these things also become a part of our story by the
deliberate use of contemporary language evocative of our
world and our times. Thus, Passover is used in parallel with
Independence Day, Jerusalem is seen as a city that over-
night could turn into a Beirut, Lebanon, in 1985; the Zealots are defined in terms of our contemporary political double
talk about "terrorists" and "freedom fighters"; the Roman
legions become "security forces" and Pilate ensures they
"keep a low profile"; Caiaphas plays cards; Jesus is seen by
the crowd "riding into town," and if that has vague over-

tones of *High Noon* about it, no damage is done, for immediately Hollywood and Jerusalem become twin cities with the qualifier "like some would-be Messiah." The vocabulary and imagery of the Bible and of our contemporary world are deliberately intermingled. Anachronism is not only tolerated but welcomed as a way of symbolizing and signifying the timelessness of the story we tell and our involvement in it.

By such simple strategies exegetical information and insights can be released from their Babylonian captivity in the conceptually-orientated, left cerebral hemisphere of the brain, and can find their appropriate homiletic expression pictured and storied in preaching. As we do that, exegesis becomes exposition, *didache* becomes *kerygma*, and we become a part of the story.

Let us take another example, this time of an exegetical insight that not only enriches our own unaided first reading of the text in our own tongue, but also uncovers new dimensions of depth in the passage that would otherwise have been missed. Take Matthew 26:6–13:

> Jesus was at Bethany in the house of Simon the leper, when a woman came to him with a small bottle of fragrant oil, very costly; and as he sat at table she began to pour it over his head. The disciples were indignant when they saw it. 'Why this waste?' they said; 'it could have been sold for a good sum and the money given to the poor.' Jesus was aware of this, and said to them, 'Why must you make trouble for the woman? It is a fine thing she has done for me. You have the poor among you always; but you will not always have me. When she poured this oil on my body it was her way of preparing me for burial. I tell you this: wherever in all the world this gospel is proclaimed, what she has done will be told as her memorial.'

At first sight this is just a very moving story about an extravagant gesture of love commended by Jesus and reminding us of our need occasionally to do extravagant things for one another and for God. All this is true, and many sermons have been preached on the subject. But if that is all that the sermon has to say it will be mere moralizing and will have missed the heart of what the passage is about. The passage is about an anointing. The word *Messiah* means "the Anointed One." So, in her extravagant gesture the woman is not just saying, "Jesus, I love you"; she is saying, "Jesus, claim your kingdom and be our King." The disciples must have known that, as Matthew's Jewish readers surely did. Yet knowing how high the stakes are, all the disciples can think of is the cost of the coronation, the waste of a year's wages in the pouring out of the oil. This is why they are rebuked. But for the woman there is no rebuke, either for her extravagance or for her daring, which could have endangered them all. Jesus celebrates what she has done and accepts the anointing, for he is indeed the Messiah. But he reminds them all that anointing is not just something done when someone is crowned, but something done when someone is buried. That is why what the woman has done was so poignantly appropriate—"it was her way of preparing me for burial," says Jesus (v. 12).

In other words Jesus embraces both meanings of anointing. He is indeed the Messiah about to go to his coronation, but his throne will be a cross and his crown a crown of thorns. He will indeed enter into the glory of his kingdom, but to enter that kingdom he must pass through the gates of death. Now we are into the meat of the passage. It is about far more than the need for us occasionally to do extravagant things for one another and for God. It is about the creative wastefulness of God in Christ on Calvary, and how, like the woman, we can take a costly share in Christ's anointing, knowing that God wastes nothing save to create or recreate. Rooted in that proclamation of what God has done we can now speak of what we ought to do without danger of mere moralizing. The text and title of the sermon might then become the disciples' question, "Why This Waste?" and the sermon might grow out of the contrast between the waste that destroys and the waste that creates—personal, societal, global, and cosmic.

We know all too well the waste that destroys . . . But we also know something of the waste that creates. In *our* creative wastefulness of time, talents, money (personal, societal, or national), we enter into the secret purposes of God. The whole physical universe from the galaxies to the atom is an extravagant gesture of God's creative love. Yet from the galaxies to the atom not one particle of energy is wasted, everything is conserved, nature recycles things, bringing new life out of death. Supremely we see God's extravagant creative love revealed in the seeming senseless waste on Calvary. Waste?! That was God's masterstroke to remake a good creation that sin had spoiled, and save a lost world. God wastes nothing save to create or recreate. He's a great saver, a great Savior.

Once again, an exegetical insight (Messiah = anointed = coronation/burial) triggers rich theological and homiletic material.

Our third example of the exegete's work as it relates to preaching is a little more difficult. This time we are concerned with the more meticulous procedures of textual criticism, including the attempt to establish the author's identity and to recover the original manuscript. Where this involves the questioning of the authorship of a much-loved passage or the rewriting of familiar verses the result can be disturbing.

I remember being dismayed when first I discovered that the story of the woman taken in adultery recorded in John 8:1–11 appeared in only one of the nine earliest manuscripts of the New Testament that we possess. Six of the others omit the story altogether, and two leave a blank space where it might be expected to appear. For this, and several other substantial reasons, many scholars question whether these verses are really a part of the Gospel John wrote, and some modern translations print John 7:53–8:11 in brackets or place it in an appendix at the end of the book. But the best contemporary scholarship seems to agree that the passage contains what Bruce Metzger calls "all the earmarks of historical veracity." Some scholars believe the story can be traced back almost as far as A.D. 100, and certainly by the fourth century Jerome's official translation of the Greek New Testament into Latin includes the passage without question. Yet for many centuries the best Greek manuscripts of Saint John's Gospel do not include this exquisite story. What is the explanation?

Augustine (354–430) is fully aware of the problem and has an intriguing answer to it. He says that the verses were omitted from many manuscripts "to avoid scandal." The church of the early centuries was at war with the secular world where sexual promiscuity had become the norm. It would be natural if church authorities were hesitant to publicize the seeming permissiveness of Jesus toward adultery, and in consequence suppressed the story. If this was what in fact happened, then these blank spaces in the Greek manuscripts can be seen as being like the not unexpected mark of censorship in the columns of a newspaper in time of war.

There are difficulties with this interpretation as with any other, but Augustine's understanding of the textual problem is not lightly to be set aside. If he is right, the exploration of the textual problem has not impoverished but enriched the story. The impact of the passage becomes all the greater as we recognize that this was a story of a forgiveness that for centuries the church thought too dangerous to be believed. Perhaps now the danger is that we too easily take it for granted! The textual criticism has turned into a part of the positive homiletic thrust of the sermon. But this is not the reason for facing the textual question. If I had come to some other conclusion I would still preach from the passage with the same love and ardor, thanking God that this blessed fragment of the Gospel, *whoever wrote it,* has been preserved for us in the Bible. Questions of authorship are important for our understanding of Scripture and must therefore be addressed honestly by the preacher. But they must never be allowed to mute our preaching, whatever the conclusion we come to, for the human authors are only the agents of the divine Author, the Holy Spirit. We must study the text of

Scripture in the security of that overarching theological conviction, knowing that if we do so reverently but rigorously the text will become for us and for those to whom we preach not less the Word of God, but more.

Of course there will be times when the exegete will veto the sermon we thought we were going to preach, but often that veto can lead us to new and richer insights. One of the earliest sermons I wrote was never preached. I was a student of philosophy at the time and theologically innocent. My text was John 8:32: "You shall know the truth, and the truth will set you free." Before I condescended to look at any commentary or theological wordbook my sermon was already well on its way, unconsciously dependent on an unlikely mix of Plato, John Locke, and David Hume. Twenty minutes of exegetical study demolished everything I had written. Not only had I wrenched the text bleeding from its context; I had also completely misunderstood what "knowing the truth" means in John's Gospel and the nature of the freedom that that knowledge brings. I remember my feeling of resentment and bereavement at the loss of that sermon, but the exegetical veto that killed it opened up for me a whole new vista of biblical understanding that soon after was radically to change and enrich not just that sermon, but my whole perception of the Christian faith. Sometimes exegetes can be our most powerful allies when they look most like our enemies.

4

The Text of Life

I have spoken of the need for thorough exegesis of the text of Scripture. Let me speak now of the need for a no less thorough exegesis of the text of life. I said at the beginning of the last chapter that the text of life (the lives we live and the world we live in) requires the same kind of exegetical and theological scrutiny that the biblical scholar brings to the text of Scripture. Just as exegesis of the text of Scripture illuminates the text of life, so exegesis of the text of life can illuminate the text of Scripture. It does so as, in the identification of the great conceptual truths of the Christian faith, we find them pictured and storied in the commonplace of human experience.

This is what Jesus himself did in the parables. He storied and pictured the doctrines he taught. Almost always he would introduce a parable by saying (either explicitly or implicitly), "I'll tell you what it's like" or "You know how it is." Then he would point to some shared commonplace of human experience. In Matthew's Gospel Jesus says over and over again, "The kingdom of heaven is like this . . ." and a story follows. With Luke it is more often an implicit "You know how it is"—you know how it is with friends at midnight, and rich fools, and guests who make excuses, and lost coins, and yeast, and so on. Even the lawyer whose question elicited the provocative parable of the Good Samaritan "knew how it was" and could answer his own question; and in the almost unbearable poignancy of the so-called parable of the Prodigal Son (surely it should be called the Hurting Father) Jesus is saying, "You know how it is between you and your children . . . how much more is it so between God and you." We must learn from Jesus. For every concept in preaching let there be a simile. Tell me what it is like, for if you cannot tell me that you probably do not know what you are talking about. If we are talking about God any simile will contain less than the whole truth, but so will any concept. Sometimes in preaching a simile can say more than a concept, not less—just as a poem can say more not less than prose. We must remember too that the most vivid similes point to familiar things that we have actually experienced. "You know how it is with your kids; 'If you know . . . how much more will your heavenly Father . . .'" (cf. Matt. 7:11).

Once again, let me try to give some specific examples of the kind of strategies we are talking about and of the way in which exegesis of life can enrich the texture of our preaching. Take this for example:

> Most of us have a rag doll in the family. It's nearly twenty years now since we adopted ours. To be more precise, Rosemary did, but we were all involved. Rosemary is my youngest child. She's in her twenties now but when first she met the rag doll she was only three. We had just flown as a family from London, England, to Melbourne, Australia. It was a long trip for a three-year-old, and when we arrived tears of exhaustion were in the child's eyes and on her cheeks. At the airport friends were waiting to greet us. One of them had brought a "welcome" gift for Rosemary, a little rag doll. She was too tired even to say "Thank you," but she clasped the rag doll to her face, hiding the tears, and the rag doll gently dried her eyes and cheeks. That night she went to bed, the rag doll still clasped tightly in her arms, still

drying the tears. The next night the tears were gone, but not the rag doll—nor the next night nor the next as days and nights turned into months and months into years. The rag doll became the most precious thing the child possessed. She had other toys intrinsically far more valuable, but none that she loved as she loved the rag doll. In time the rag doll became more rag than doll and began to get a bit dirty. Cleaning was a problem, for that made it more ragged still. The sensible thing to do was to face the fact that the rag doll had never been worth much and was now no more than a bundle of dirty rags that ought to be trashed. But that was unthinkable for anyone who loved my child. If you loved Rosemary, you had to love the rag doll. That was part of the package.

The story is a commonplace. There is hardly a family without a rag doll in it. The rag doll is Linus's blanket in "Peanuts," Radar's teddy bear in "M*A*S*H," and the Velveteen Rabbit all rolled into one. What we can easily overlook is that it is theologically loaded! Here is the *agape* love that does not look for value in what it loves as *eros* love does, but that creates value there. Here are echoes of Isaiah 64:6, "We all became like a man who is unclean and all our righteous deeds like a filthy rag"; of Romans 3:23, "All alike have sinned, and are deprived of the divine splendour, and all are justified by God's free grace alone." Here, embedded in a commonplace, we find our commonplace selves.

We are God's rag dolls, intrinsically worthless, trash if you like, yet precious beyond all computing because we have been loved to life by one who says, "Love me, love my rag dolls." "If a man says, 'I love God', while hating his brother, he is a liar" (1 John 4:20). "Love the Lord your God . . . and your neighbor as yourself" (Matt. 22:36–39; Mark 12:29–31, Luke 10:25–28). God, neighbor, and self are all part of the package, and that's why those who love God dare not trash anyone, not even themselves.

The material still has to be homiletically organized, but a

hermeneutic transaction has already been carried through that has turned the conceptual insights of a word study on *eros* and *agape* and the tough theological concepts of imputed righteousness and justification by faith into doctrine that has been pictured, storied, and readied for the pulpit. Of course in some ways the simile of the rag doll has said less than the concepts of a word study or a theological statement would have done; that is why, as we shall be emphasizing shortly, the conceptual structure must always be strong and clearly defined. But in some ways and for some people I believe the simile says more, not less, than the concept. And, because everyone knows about rag dolls, this simile can say not only "God's love is like that"; it can also say with assurance to all of us who know about rag dolls, "You know what it's like—you know what *God's* kind of love is like; for all of us have seen that kind of loving, and we know that it does not look for value in what it loves, but by loving creates value."

This kind of thing is what I mean by "exegesis of life." That phrase is a piece of clumsy gobbledegook. It denotes what is usually described more simply as sermon illustration. I hate gobbledegook and much prefer to describe things simply—especially when preaching. But by "exegesis of life" I mean more than illustration. Through exegesis of life we discover that in the text of life is embedded the same revelation of God in Christ that is given to us in the text of Scripture. We can identify that revelation only through the text of Scripture, but what we identify is not just an illustration of scriptural truth, it is a part of that truth. I believe it is not by accident that the story of the rag doll is so highly charged theologically. If we really believe that our crucified Carpenter is the agent of all creation—including rag dolls and the children who love them—then we must expect to find anywhere, everywhere, the handwriting of the Author of both the text of Scripture and the text of life—God in Christ revealing himself to us through the power of the Spirit.

Often the preacher searches desperately for illustrations, sometimes falling back on books of illustrations. The best of these can sometimes be helpful. The worst of them turn out to be anthologies containing innumerable wildly dramatic and improbable stories, each indexed and offered to illustrate whatever anyone may want to say about anything. This can encourage a tiresomely predictable sermon where secondhand illustrations are used indiscriminately to punctuate the sermon at five-minute intervals, often doing more harm than good. Sometimes what claim to be "true stories" sound untrue and no doubt are. This effectively illustrates nothing except the questionable truth of anything else the preacher may have to say. Sometimes the story illustrates the obvious, which is merely boring. Sometimes the story illustrates interestingly and well something the sermon is not talking about, and accordingly, though interesting, is digressive.

I think we should be less obsessive in our search for stories and start looking harder at the real world about us. All around us in the commonplace of our shared experience the text of life lies waiting to yield to the exegete of life the theological riches it contains. Like those who first heard the gospel preached, we live in a world of friends at midnight, rich fools, guests who make excuses, lost coins, yeast, Good Samaritans, and hurting parents—and rag dolls (1 John 4:20), and innumerable other commonplace profundities. The teaching of Jesus clearly shows us the way, and we must learn more faithfully to follow. The world is full of rag dolls and the like, trivial yet tremendous truths that are the fruits of reverent, rigorous "exegesis of life."

I find that, once students get the feel of this kind of exegesis and know where to look for it, they discover that theological and homiletic riches begin to tumble into their laps. I remember a student who was an excellent golfer. He preached a sermon on Romans 5:8–9. (It is not immediately apparent what Romans 5 has to do with golf, but rag dolls and the like turn up in the most unexpected places.)

But God shows his love for us in that while we were yet sinners Christ died for us. Since, therefore, we are now justified by his blood, much more shall we be saved by him from the wrath of God. [Rom. 5:8–9, RSV]

It was a hard text for anyone to preach. He was speaking about God's love and forgiveness in Christ and how we are "justified by his blood" (that was the really tough bit). He was wrestling with the seeming paradox that God's love and forgiveness are absolute and unconditional, yet no less absolute in their demand on us.

He told a story from his own boyhood. He used to spend hours in the back yard practicing his golf swing. Of course he wasn't allowed to use a real golf ball because that could be very dangerous so near to the house, and also could be expensive in lost balls. So he used a practice ball—hollow and made of light plastic with holes in it. You couldn't hit it far and it could do no damage. One day he thought that both his parents were out and the house empty, and he longed for the feel of a real golf ball on the head of a club. At this point we in the congregation all thought we knew what was coming and were enjoying it. Sure enough, he sliced his stroke and the ball swung inexorably toward his parents' bedroom window. We were ready to laugh. Then suddenly the whole mood changed. He was still speaking quietly and undramatically, but he said:

I heard the glass shatter and then I heard my mother scream. I ran into the house and up the stairs to her bedroom. She was standing there in front of the broken window and she was bleeding. I started to cry and I couldn't stop, and all I could say was, "Mum, what have I done, I could have killed you." I don't know how often I said it. And she kept just hugging me and saying, "It's all right, I'm all right, everything's going to be all right."

We in the congregation were not laughing anymore when he

said, "After that, I could never again take a real golf ball into the back yard."

Then he spoke once more of Romans 5:8–9, of that unconditional love and forgiveness God showed to us "while we were yet sinners," of how we are justified (put right with God) by Christ's blood, of how all we can say is "What have I done? I could have killed you," of how Christ embraces us in our Easter faith and says, "It's all right, I'm all right, everything's going to be all right." Then he added, "After you've seen that, after you've heard him say that, you know there are some things you can never do again in the back yard or anywhere else." It is worth identifying what the student has done. He has taken a biblical concept, "God's love is absolute and unconditional, yet no less absolute in its demand," and he has found for that concept a simile that not only instructs our intellect but touches our heart and empowers our will. The result was a fine sermon, deeply rooted in the text of Scripture and of life, the imperative of Christian ethics empowered by the indicative of Christian theology, what we ought to do made possible by what God has done.

The raw material for the exegesis of life is everywhere. Sometimes that fact seems to be better understood on Madison Avenue than it is on our seminary campuses. A careful study of television commercials is an interesting exercise for the preacher. Usually commercials tell us a lot more about ourselves than they do about the products they advertise. Often what they tell us is unflattering. The careful research that lies behind many commercials signals clearly that, whatever else we are or are not, we are greedy, lustful, and selfish. It is these unlovely characteristics of human nature that the advertiser identifies and seeks to exploit. On other occasions our hopes and fears, joys and sorrows are all being explored and often exploited, and in that exploration not infrequently "the children of this world" on Madison Avenue prove to be more perceptive than we "children of light" on our seminary campuses (Luke 16:8, KJV). Sometimes there can be an exuberant celebration of the enjoyment of life in the brash "things go better with Coke" kind of commercials. There is no need to be brash about it but Jesus did say that he came so that we might have life "in all its fullness" (John 10:10). Not infrequently a deeper level of human experience is revealed in these commercials. Fragments of trivial conversation are heard—intimate, tender, funny, excited, poignant, loving—concluding always with the same jingle, "Reach out and touch someone." That commercial did very well for the Bell Telephone Company over many years. The image of reaching out and touching is primitive, powerful, and rich. It is also psychologically, ethically, and evangelistically suggestive—and theologically loaded as well, to those who believe that God in Christ has reached out and touched our world (see Mark 1:41). As I write, a similar commercial is doing splendidly selling a brand of instant coffee. Tiny vignettes are played out between two people—husband and wife, parent and child, teacher and pupil. For example, an attractive, middle-aged couple are sitting quietly by the fire holding hands. The camera looks lovingly around a pleasant room, passing lightly over some family photographs, then back to the woman's face. She's got a faraway look in her eyes and she's smiling. "What are you thinking about?" the man asks. She answers, "I was just thinking how good life is." The man says very tenderly (guess what?), "I'll go make some coffee." And then the music fades in with the jingle superimposed, "Times like these are made [to share Brand X]," and a jar of instant coffee appears on the television screen. Pure corn! Yet this is not just sentimental rubbish. Production standards are high, and the acting is competent in this thirty-second docu-drama.

"Times like these" are, thank God, a part of the experience of each one of us—times of deep joy at nothing in particular and everything in general, times that deserve to be celebrated with more than a cup of instant coffee. These are thanksgiving times, Eucharist times, bread-and-wine times maybe, but not just coffee breaks. Commonplace joys and sorrows, hopes and fears, faith and doubt, pleasures and pains, glories and shames are all part of the rich texture of our shared human experience. As we explore that experience reverently and rigorously we become exegetes of life. The real world in which we live becomes a revelation of God in Christ as we identify what he is doing here and now through what he did once for all, there and then, as recorded in the Scriptures of the Old and the New Testaments.

When we set side by side the text of Scripture and the text of life we are at once aware of similarities and parallels too numerous and suggestive to be merely accidental. We preach in the conviction that the same God is revealed in both texts and in each is telling the same story. Yet, in spite of the similarities, the preacher is often frustrated to find that there are stubborn incongruities between the two texts. We know the texts belong together, yet they do not exactly fit. That is when we are tempted to cheat. In the interest of clarity we distort the text of Scripture just a little to make it fit more exactly the text of life; or else we distort the text of life just a little to make it fit more exactly the text of Scripture; or else (trying to be fair) we distort both texts and hope no one will notice. Even when our tampering goes undetected and the desired clarity is achieved the sermon usually stays flat, and I think we can see why.

I believe the homiletic perspective involves a kind of binocular vision. Notice what happens when we open both our eyes and look at the physical world about us. Our two eyes see two images, suggestively similar but not wholly congruent. Each eye sees the world from a slightly different perspective. One would expect the result to be a blurring of vision, like two photographs superimposed the one on the other, both of the same object but each taken from a slightly different angle. But when we use both our eyes we find not only that the two images presented to our consciousness have fused without blurring into a single image, but also that our binocular vision enables us to see the world about us in a new dimension of depth. With only one eye it is much harder to judge distance, to see things accurately in depth, than it is with two eyes.

When we look at the text of Scripture and the text of life, and become conscious not only of the suggestive similarities but of the minor incongruities they represent, we must not distort either text. We must look honestly at both, knowing that if we do the Spirit-given moment will come when the two texts will fuse into one and we shall begin to see both in new dimensions of depth. I believe such a moment of insight occurred for me in the preparation of a sermon on Matthew 26:6–13 which we discussed earlier (see pp. 41–43). At first the reference to burial (Matt. 26:12) did not quite "fit" what I wanted the passage to say, so I tried to ignore it. Then I realized that the seeming incongruity was the key to a deeper perception not only of the text of Scripture but of the text of life as well. The preacher reads the text of Scripture as an exegete and the text of life as a pastor; but the two texts are read together, creating a kind of binocular vision that can see both texts as one without either distortion or confusion. That is the unique homiletic perspective of an authentically biblical preacher.

5

Organic Unity

Sermons are more like babies than buildings. We do not really construct them—they grow in us. Often sermons are thought of as constructs and homiletics is seen as the art of sermon construction. Students of homiletics are taught how to be good architects. The text of Scripture and the text of life will provide them with the raw materials out of which they will design and make something. Preacher-architects are expected to be in control of their material and to know what they are doing. All that is very sensible; the preacher has much to learn from the architect, and that is why books on sermon construction and sermon design have much to teach us. But I believe that that image of construction and architecture is less than adequate to describe what happens in preparing a sermon. The best sermons are not just things that we design and make; rather, they are things that grow in us and eventually are delivered by us, but (dare we say it!) are conceived by the Holy Spirit. Sometimes in greater or lesser degree I believe that all of us experience in our sermon preparation an identifiable, creative moment of miraculous conception in which we can echo Ezekiel's favorite words, "The word of the Lord came to me"; and with Mary can respond, "As you have spoken, so be it" (Luke

1:26–38). These are the moments in which we know that something God-given has been conceived in us and is beginning to grow.

From that first moment of conception through its embryonic development, the sermon is a part of us, and yet it has a mysterious life of its own. Sometimes we have to go through painful and protracted labor before the living thing that is growing in us is ready to face the world and can safely be delivered. For most of us the delivery itself is not easy, often terrifying; "but when the child is born [we] forget the anguish" (John 16:21). Looked at this way, the relationship between preachers and their sermons is more like that of a mother to a child than of an architect to a building. There is a sense in which an architect may have "conceived" a building; mothers conceive in a more intimate and more literal way. Our sermons, like our children, are a part of us. That is why we spring to their defense in the face of any threat or criticism. We are quite prepared to admit that sometimes they can be awful, but we do not like to see other people roughing them up. That is what makes the teaching of homiletics such a delicate task. No parent of a newborn child wants to hear anything about the baby except that it is the most beautiful baby in the world.

Thinking of a sermon as an organism rather than as a construct has certain important implications for the preacher, and it is to these that we now turn.

Thinking of a sermon as an organism points to the need for organic unity. Both in its literal and in its metaphorical sense the word *organism* is descriptive of something characterized by a diversity of function contained within an overarching unity of structure. Paul uses the metaphor of organism to express the functional diversity contained within the organic unity of the church. The metaphor is boldly extended when he speaks of the church as "the body of Christ."

For just as in a single human body there are many limbs and organs, all with different functions, so all of us, united with Christ, form one body, serving individually as limbs and organs to one another. [Rom. 12:4–5]

The same image is further extended in 1 Corinthians:

> For Christ is like a single body with its many limbs and organs, which, many as they are, together make up one body. . . . A body is not one single organ, but many. . . . If the whole were one single organ, there would not be a body at all. . . . God has combined the various parts of the body, . . . that there might be no sense of division in the body. . . . Now you are Christ's body, and each of you a limb or organ of it. [1 Cor. 12:12–27]

I believe that what is true of the church is also true of the church's preaching. A sermon may indeed have many limbs and organs, but together, many as they are, they are one body. Organic unity is a prerequisite of efficient functioning for all developed forms of life. Babies born as twins live full, happy, and independent lives because they are two separate babies, not one, and are free to be themselves and to go their own way. But Siamese twins can never live full lives until they have been separated by the surgeon's knife. Some three-point sermons are really Siamese triplets in disguise—three separate infants, each with its own small body, its own organic unity, each with a capacity for vigorous development, but each frustrated by the others in its capacity to grow and go places. For such sadly misconceived sermons radical surgery is the only answer.

Always look for the beating heart of the sermon, using for your guide the theme sentence and purpose statement that are the distillation of your exegetical work on the text of Scripture (see pp. 37–38). Explore that theme and develop that purpose in the text of life (see chap. 4), and let the sermon grow at the point where the two stories and the two texts intersect (see chaps. 2–4). Keep tightening the focus of your insight into both stories and into both texts. That way a dim, diffused beam that illuminates nothing in particular can turn into a bright spotlight or even a laser beam that can probe the depths of our inner space. Write and rewrite that theme sentence and purpose statement as your insight deepens. Do not try to *impose* shape on the living thing you are bringing to birth. You will only damage the fetus. Let it grow until you can *discover* the shape of the living thing that God is bringing to life in you. The final draft of your theme sentence and purpose statement should identify the heart of the sermon and reflect the organic unity that will determine its shape. Be absolutely sure that your theme and purpose are deeply rooted both in the text of Scripture and in the text of life. Then let your sermon be about that *and nothing else*. Read again at this point what was said on pages 23–24 about the two meanings of the word *expository,* a narrower meaning describing a sermon's form and a wider meaning describing its content. The procedure I am describing now is expository in the wider theological sense, where expository preaching and biblical preaching are seen to be the same thing. (Verse-by-verse Bible study will, of course, employ other strategies.)

Organic unity in a sermon not only tolerates but requires a multiplicity of interdependent functions—Paul's "many limbs and organs." The heart of an organism cannot live without the body any more than a body can live without a heart. The heart of a sermon is identified by its theme sentence and purpose statement. (The theme sentence for the rag-doll sermon was "God's love doesn't look for value but creates value." The purpose of the sermon was to reactivate the familiar text "If God so loves us we ought also to love one another.") The heart begins to beat only as it becomes "embodied" in the text of Scripture and the text of life. This happens as the abstract indicative of the theme sentence becomes increasingly concrete, and as the general imperative of the purpose statement becomes increasingly specific. In that process we begin to identify the interdependent functions of the various parts of the body. *The sermon needs to have a skeleton, a cardiovascular system, flesh, and muscle.*

The skeleton of a sermon is its conceptual structure. The intellectual framework must be strong, and what is said must be intellectually honest and rationally defensible. We are all tempted at times to cut intellectual corners. The pulpit lifts us several feet above contradiction, and our congregations have been well-conditioned into not talking back—except with a devout "amen" or "hallelujah." That can offer us a license to cheat, and we must resist the temptation to accept it. We must bring to bear on what we are saying all that we have learned in our schools of theology about biblical studies, systematics, and the rest, not forgetting the harder lessons most of us have learned in the school of life. Preaching must be intellectually honest, and consequently the conceptual skeleton must be strong. But in a healthy body not all of the bone structure is visible. Some sermons have excellent skeletons but little else. At best that means that they are too thin, at worst it means that they ought to be decently buried.

Some skeletons are invertebrate—they have no backbone. It is true that invertebrate creatures can live a normal, healthy life, but it is usually a primitive form of life. A worm is invertebrate. I am told (though I have never put it to the test) that you can cut a worm in two, and the two halves will wriggle off quite happily in different directions. I know little about worms, but I have known many sermons like that. You could chop the preacher off at ten minutes, or twenty, or thirty, or forty, and it wouldn't really matter very much. The bits of the invertebrate sermon would still wriggle off quite happily in different directions. Sermons, being more than primitive life forms, ought to be vertebrate organisms, each part of the body dependent upon the organic unity of the whole. If you cut a vertebrate organism in two you kill it.

Some bone structures cause a lot of pain because they are arthritic—the joints don't work effectively. Arthritic sermons are disjointed. The transitions from one thought cluster to another are made clumsily or not at all, and in consequence the argument is confused and obscure. I spend a great deal of time working on transitions, working out exactly how one thought cluster is to be jointed with what has come immediately before it and with what will immediately succeed it. The joint must work smoothly. There is little value in a sermon having a strong conceptual skeleton if every movement it makes is painful.

The cardiovascular system or bloodstream is the emotive flow of the sermon. Every counselor knows that what we feel is often more important than what we think, and in consequence the emotive cardiovascular system of a sermon is certainly no less important than the conceptual skeleton. Indeed, cardiovascular disease, in sermons as in people, causes more fatalities than broken bones do. When the truth communicated in preaching is only thought to be true but not felt to be true, we have not heard the full gospel. The Bible does not tolerate the separation of the head from the heart (see chap. 8). The heart has its *reasons*. Felt truths are not to be despised. Preaching involves a kind of passionate thinking. Sometimes the preacher is giving conceptual expression to what the hearer had previously only felt to be true; but sometimes the preacher is expressing as a felt truth something the hearer had previously only thought to be true. Both tasks are equally important, and for both a healthy cardiovascular system is required that can express felt truths and carry the affect (the feel) of these truths to every limb and organ of the sermon. This is the lifeblood of preaching.

Felt truths are communicated as we picture and story concepts. Take, for example, the following passage on the meaning of faith *(pistis)* and love *(agape)* in the New Testament. It is quoted from an article by C. E. B. Cranfield in Alan Richardson's *Theological Word Book of the Bible*. The material is expressed with admirable economy and lucidity, and in purely conceptual terms—as is appropriate in a theological wordbook article. The tone is cool and clinical. But this is homiletic dynamite.

It is clear that "love to God" and "faith" largely overlap.
Both denote the response to the divine love. It is noticeable
that though often speaking of the divine love and of love between Christians, Paul rarely speaks of the Christian's
love to God. Nygren argues from this that Paul avoided using love in this sense on principle, because he was fixing
agape as a technical term for the spontaneous, uncaused
love (God's love to men and its extension in our love to
neighbors), and so did not want to use the same term of our
love to God, which is essentially *caused,* not spontaneous.
Nygren's view is that Paul uses *pistis* (faith) to denote what
in the Synoptics is love to God . . . . Though undoubtedly
right in his general thesis, Nygren is perhaps rather doctri-
naire in pressing this distinction between Paul and the
Synoptics. In this connection it is interesting to note that
Barth ("Kirchliche Dogmatik", 1/2, pp. 435f.) can see a similarity between God's love to us and ours to him, that makes
the use of the same term for both appropriate (*Theological
Word Book of the Bible,* ed. Richardson, p. 135).

That near equation between faith and love opens up for
the preacher suggestive insights into the meaning of justification by faith. Faith does not mean merely intellectual assent, nor does justification mean being made just.
Justification means to be brought into a right relationship
with somebody. The substitution of the word *love* for "faith"
as the agent of our justification opens up a new perspective
for the preacher on the theological concept as it does on texts
traditionally associated with the concept. For example, "all
bec[o]me like a man who is unclean and all our righteous
deeds like a filthy rag" (Isa. 64:6) or "all alike have sinned,
and are deprived of the divine splendour, and all are justified by God's free grace alone" (Rom. 3:23–24).

At this point the prophet's simile of the filthy rag brings
the rag doll into the story (see pp. 47–49). The concept of the
wordbook article on *agape* and *eros* is reduced to its simplest
form. "Some things are loved because they are valuable, but
some things are valued because they are loved"; we become
God's rag doll; "love me, love my rag dolls" becomes a para-

phrase of 1 John 4:20 and of the Great Commandment. The image of the rag doll is now in the bloodstream of the sermon and appears again and again in natural association with other images of love and tears, and getting filthy and trying to get ourselves clean; and in the end, one hopes, we understand just a little better the meaning of imputed righteousness and justification by faith. "God's free grace alone" affirms our infinite worth and puts us right with him and with one another. The difference between *agape* and *eros* and the similarity between *agape* and *pistis* is the exegetical conceptual backbone of the sermon, the product of the logical, analytic, dispassionate so-called left hemisphere of the brain. But preaching can never be *merely* logical, analytic, and dispassionate. In the rag doll the concept finds its appropriate simile and the simile permeates the bloodstream of the sermon. The simile is the product of the analogical, synthetic, passionate so-called right hemisphere of the brain that pictures and stories doctrine as Jesus did. The right hemisphere stimulates the sermon's cardiovascular system and keeps it healthy.

The flesh of the sermon is the "incarnation" of its theme. To be incarnate is to be made flesh, and every sermon needs to be fleshed out. Let us see what that means in relation to the *agape* theme we have been discussing. The heart of the sermon will be the theme sentence, "God's love does not look for value but creates value." The conceptual skeleton will be structured on the difference between *agape* and *eros* (and the similarity between *agape* and *pistis*). *Agape* love is pictured and storied in the rag doll, and that will become the key simile in the sermon's cardiovascular system. Let us now see how all this might be fleshed out. Two preliminary warnings, however, are necessary. First, we must not confuse fleshing out with "padding." Flesh is living tissue, part of the organic unity that constitutes the sermon as a whole; padding can be made of almost any material and is there only to make the sermon seem a little more substantial than it really is. Second, we must always be careful in "fleshing out" not to allow the sermon to become flabby and overweight. Many sermons are in more need of slimming down than of fleshing out. Nevertheless, without fleshing out, the skeleton and the cardiovascular system will go nowhere fast. The need for that "enfleshment" is not just a recognition of the communication-skills requirement to make the abstract concrete; it is a recognition of a theological requirement in the communication of Christian truth. Truth fleshed out is truth incarnate. God's truth, once perfectly incarnate conclusively in the Word made flesh, can become in the Word preached a new incarnation, however imperfect. How else can we believe that "the preaching of the Word is the Word of God" (see pp. 14, 16)?

Let us now consider how the sermon about *agape* love and the rag doll might be fleshed out.

1. We have already seen that *we* are God's rag dolls—the *agape* concept and the story have already become incarnate in us (see pp. 48–49).
2. Notice further how people become lovable by being loved and identify in that the "enfleshment" of John's words, "We love because he loved us first" (1 John 4:19).
3. All of us live in the blessed assurance that some people love us, not because of our virtues, but in spite of our faults. We can see that as an "enfleshment" of "the love I speak of is not our love for God but the love he showed to us in sending his Son to be the remedy for the defilement of our sins."
4. Identify the ecclesial, social, national, and global dimensions of the theme, especially as they relate to John's "if a man says, 'I love God', while hating his brother, he is a liar" (1 John 4:20).

By now the sermon is almost certainly overweight. Our task is no longer to flesh it out but to slim it down. But notice that none of the material is mere padding. All of it is living tissue that has grown out of the organic unity of the theme and is a natural development of the theme sentence, "Some things are loved because they are valuable, but some things are valuable because they are loved." And all of this material has grown out of the concept of *agape* love as pictured and storied in the rag doll.

The muscle of the sermon is that part of it that requires and enables action. Every sermon is, explicitly or implicitly, an invitation to pilgrimage, a call for commitment or recommitment. Sometimes that invitation is explicit and structured. In the liturgical traditions of the church where the Eucharist is celebrated every Sunday, the invitation to approach the altar rail as a response to the Word of God is explicit and structured. The same is true of the nonliturgical evangelical practice where the regular "altar call" is no less explicit and no less structured, as the worshipers are invited to "come forward" in response to the hearing of the Word. In yet other traditions (my own included) that moment of response, decision, and commitment is often left implicit and unstructured. That can be both a weakness and a strength, but, whether the response to the Word is made explicit or left implicit, the preacher dare never forget that the preaching event is always incomplete without some kind of response. We may or may not move from our seats, but in some way our response to the Word must involve some change in our posture, some change in the way we think and feel and act, some change in the way we see ourselves and one another and God.

That change is what the New Testament means by the word *metanoia,* the word we usually translate "repentance." But when we speak of repentance we must remember that *metanoia* means much more than feeling remorseful about the wrong things we have done (though it often includes that). It means a reorientation that changes and enriches our relationship with God and with one another. That is why always, even when we are "preaching to the converted," we are in a real sense still preaching for conversion. The word *conversion* occurs only once in most English Bibles (Acts

15:3). The word so translated is *epistrophe,* a word more often translated "turning" or "returning." It is closely related in meaning to the much more familiar word *metanoia* which, as we have just seen, is usually translated "repentance" but which is perhaps more accurately rendered "a change of attitude" or "a change of heart." These word clusters—*metanoia*/repentance/change of attitude, and *epistrophe*/conversion/turning or returning—lie at the heart of Christian experience. The muscle power of preaching is gauged by its capacity to change attitudes (that is what repentance means) and to turn human lives around (that is what conversion means). At the end of any sermon the question must be asked, "So what?"—why have you told me all this, what now are you asking me to do or not to do, in what way is what you have said meant to change my attitude or turn my life around? "What must I *do* to be saved?" (Acts 16:30). If the response to these questions is tentative or evasive, the sermon lacks muscle.

It is important, however, to remember that what gives a sermon muscle is not simply the demand for action; rather it is the insight that enables the action. Read again pages 18–20 and 21–22. Note especially the last sentence of the chapter: "[Authentic biblical preaching] is about action enabled by insight, imperatives empowered by indicatives, ethics rooted in theology, 'what we ought to do' made possible by what God has done." The rag doll is helpful because it turns out to be a surprisingly muscular character. Read again the rag-doll quotation on page 48. The imperatives are inescapable, and in the sermon they will of course be "fleshed out" in specifics. But they are imperatives that are empowered by the indicatives of the gospel, Christian ethics rooted in Christian theology, "what we ought to do" made possible by what God has done.

Let us take one final example of what I mean by muscle in a sermon, again, for the sake of economy, drawing on material already quoted. Read again pages 50–52. The student's sermon on Romans 5:8–9 had already fleshed out the "re-

pentance" dimension of the theme. "Christ died for us while
we were yet sinners" became "What have I done, I could
have killed you." Then he did the same for the central keryg-
matic dimension. "Justified by Christ's sacrificial death, we
shall . . . be saved" became Good Friday, Easter, and parousia in "It's all right, I'm all right, everything's going to be
all right." In consequence there was no mere moralizing or
false pietism when finally the student turned to the "conversion" dimension and spoke very specifically of "things
we can never do again in the back yard or anywhere else"
after we "repent" and "believe the gospel." There is muscle in
that material. A guilty conscience may be all that is necessary to require action, but it takes real muscle to enable it.

We began this chapter on organic unity by quoting Paul's
image of "a single human body with many limbs and organs, all with different functions." We end the chapter with
a parallel image from Ezekiel, but this time the question is
not "How is a living body structured?" but "What gives a
structured body life?"

The hand of the LORD came upon me, and he carried me
out by his spirit and put me down in a plain full of bones. He
made me go to and fro across them until I had been round
them all; they covered the plain, countless numbers of
them, and they were very dry. He said to me, 'Man, can
these bones live again?' I answered, 'Only thou knowest
that, Lord GOD.' He said to me, 'Prophesy over these bones
and say to them, O dry bones, hear the word of the LORD.
This is the word of the Lord GOD to these bones: I will put
breath into you, and you shall live. I will fasten sinews on
you, bring flesh upon you, overlay you with skin, and put
breath in you, and you shall live; and you shall know that I
am the LORD.' I began to prophesy as he had bidden me, and
as I prophesied there was a rustling sound and the bones
fitted themselves together. As I looked, sinews appeared
upon them, flesh covered them, and they were overlaid with
skin, but there was no breath in them. Then he said to me,
'Prophesy to the wind, prophesy, man, and say to it, These

are the words of the Lord GOD: Come, O wind, come from
every quarter and breathe into these slain, that they may
come to life.' I began to prophesy as he had bidden me:
breath came into them; they came to life and rose to their
feet, a mighty host. [Ezek. 37:1–10]

Ezekiel is talking about Israel just as Paul was talking
about the church, but either of them could equally well have
been talking about preaching. Of course it is exciting for us
preachers when the bones of our sermons begin to come together and flesh and sinew cover them and they really look
quite presentable creatures. But sometimes I have had an
uneasy feeling with some of my own sermons that though
they looked all right "there was [still] no breath in them."
That is when we need to remember the work of the Holy
Spirit. We believe that sermons are conceived in us by the
Spirit (see p. 56) and that the same Spirit is with us from the
time of conception through maturation to the time of delivery. In a later chapter we shall try to translate that claim
from a pious generalization into the particularities of sermon preparation. Meantime we can simply thank God that
often we have heard and sometimes we have preached sermons where "breath came into them; they came to life and
rose to their feet . . ."

6

How Sermons Grow

Getting Started

This is often the hardest part. How do we decide what passage we shall preach from and on what theme? Often we can be paralyzed by the multiple choices that confront us. What one thing is it that God wants us to say in this one sermon, on this particular Sunday?

In some traditions a lectionary, prescribing the passages to be read on any given Sunday, automatically narrows the choice. The value of a lectionary is very great. It saves us from constant danger of becoming locked inside our own personal canon and compels us to preach on passages and themes we might otherwise have ignored. It also is an invaluable aid in getting started. We are immediately directed toward specific passages and can therefore quickly get down to exegetical business (see pp. 37–38). One caveat only is required for those for whom the lectionary is normative. Often three passages are prescribed—Old Testament, Epistle, and Gospel. Sometimes the link between the three is tenuous or nonexistent. It is better to preach well on one passage than badly on all three. The passages not preached

on can be read, but should not be force-fed into the sermon if
the sermon cannot naturally digest and assimilate them.

Some traditions (my own included) provide a lectionary,
but do not require it to be followed in public worship. I think
all preacher-pastors would do well to require of themselves
that they follow some lectionary discipline for their own private devotional enrichment. Sometimes passages so read
catch fire immediately and demand to be preached. But
even when this does not happen, the time given to Bible
reading will have been well spent in the deepening of the
preacher's own devotional life and hence the preparing of
the subsoil for future sermons.

Even when the lectionary is not part of the preacher's tradition, the great festivals of the Christian year often are—
Advent, Christmas, Epiphany, Lent, Holy Week, Easter,
Ascension, Pentecost, Trinity. The rhythm of the Christian
year carries the preacher through the great central doctrines of the faith. The Christian seasons, like the lectionary, choose the theme for us. (Who, otherwise, would be
able to guarantee at least one sermon a year on the ascension or on the Trinity?) In consequence the range of our
preaching is widened; we escape from our subjective canons
and agendas and turn immediately to one of the appropriate
passages for the day. Like the lectionary preacher we can
quickly get down to exegetical business. To the great themes
of the Christian year the secular calendar makes its own
counterpoint—New Year, Memorial Day, Mother's Day, Independence Day, Labor Day, Thanksgiving Day, and the rest.
On special days such as these the preacher is again relieved
of the paralyzing burden of choice that can often make it so
hard to get started on an "ordinary" Sunday.

For most of us, however, most Sundays are "ordinary"
Sundays, and (unless the lectionary is normative) the burden of multiple choice will remain. Sermon series are a
blessed lifeline to sanity. When I was required to prepare at
least two sermons every week, one of the two would almost
always be part of a series. The options are obvious and in-

finitely rich—the Lord's Prayer, the Commandments, the
Beatitudes, the parables, a series of sermons on a single
epistle such as Philippians, a series on Old Testament
narrative like the Joseph story, a series on the minor
prophets, a series on the Psalms, a series on the Apostles'
Creed—these are only a few random samples of the kind of
thing that kept me sane and even sanguine during many
tough years as a pastor-preacher. The choice of possible sermon series is almost as wide as the choice of possible sermons. But once a choice is made the burden of weekly choice
is lifted from the preacher's shoulders. Getting started is no
longer a problem. In addition, time spent on exegetical preparation for a series of sermons can be more highly concen-
trated, more thorough, and less time-consuming than
similar work done for a single sermon. The same exegetical
insights will inform not just one sermon but many.

At the same time, I find it necessary always to leave in
the preaching schedule plenty of space for the "one-off" sermon—for "the word of the Lord that came to me" unbidden,
unplanned, and unscheduled. How do these sermons get
started, and how can we be sure that they keep coming?
(Many of us have a secret fear that one day we shall simply
dry up.) In the preparation of any one sermon I find that I am
constantly having to inhibit digressions in order to main-
tain the organic unity of the whole. But these inhibited digressions, if they contain potentially valuable material, are
not discarded. They are carefully recorded in a pocket notebook that goes with me everywhere. That notebook is like a
seedbed in which seminal material is carefully stored and
given time to strike roots so that it can take on a life of its
own. Thus, in the preparation of one sermon, the seeds of
several others may be sown. The completion of one sermon
should leave the preacher's mind not barren but pregnant
with possibilities for others. Getting started on the next sermon no longer means the desolating experience of facing a
blank page with a blank mind. It means rather the intriguing experience of exploring the seedbed to see what is going

on there. "A man scatters seed on the land; he goes to bed at night and gets up in the morning, and the seed sprouts and grows—how, he does not know" (Mark 4:26–27). Even while we sleep creative things are happening, things are growing, and in God's good time will come to harvest.

But the pocket notebook contains far more than inhibited digressions gleaned from times of sermon preparation. All that has been said already in chapters 3 and 4 about exegesis of the text of Scripture and exegesis of the text of life depends on our developing that homiletic perspective, that binocular vision, that turns sight into insight and yields perception in depth in both texts (see pp. 54–55). These moments of insight can come any time and any place—not just in the study. Usually they do not come as a blinding revelation, just as a small, arresting, delighted "Aha!" We may not yet know precisely what has arrested and delighted us or what it is going to become. But we must at once put it safely in the notebook, plant it carefully in the seedbed. Many of our moments of insight come to nothing and die. But many take root and grow. Every time we read the text of Scripture or the text of life it can happen. It is happening all the time. God is revealing himself in his Word and in this world. Our everyday experience is punctuated by theophanies. We must keep looking for the transcendent in the trivial, and, when we glimpse it, we must grab that pocket notebook! A dozen words miraculously conceived in the supermarket can sometimes be worth much more than many pages of immaculate typescript ill-conceived in the study.

Depending on our temperament and tradition any or all of these procedures can help us to get started.

Thinking and Praying

At this stage in our discussion homiletic generalities become increasingly dangerous. What works for one person fails miserably for another. All I can do is describe what seems to work for me and for many of the students and pastors I teach. I am assuming now that we have reached the stage where we know what passage we are going to preach on and have followed the exegetical procedures outlined on pages 37–38. Now what?

Think! That seems offensively obvious. But I believe that many of us spend too large a proportion of our sermon-preparation time in reading and writing and not enough time in thinking. We have understood what we have read about the passage and its theme, but we have not given it much thought. What we have read and what we shall ultimately say have not become a part of our way of thinking and speaking. This means we have not adequately internalized what we are saying. In order to internalize a sermon we must think it through from beginning to end again and again. And, if that has to mean a little less time for reading and writing, then so be it!

And *pray!* What we say in preaching becomes a part of us only if we have given it a lot of that special kind of thinking where thinking and praying become almost indistinguishable. Thoughts turn naturally into prayers and prayers into thought. Sometimes the devotional element in our sermon preparation can degenerate into little more than variations on the theme "God, give me a sermon." We would do better to pray with the Book of Hours of 1514:

> God be in my head and in my understanding;
> God be in my eyes and in my looking;
> God be in my mouth and in my speaking;
> God be in my heart and in my thinking . . .

And, since we preachers should never forget our fragility and mortality, we do well to finish the prayer.

> God be at my end and at my departing.

That old prayer perfectly reflects the kind of thinking-praying that we preachers must consciously try to cultivate. Such prayer is not just pietistical, and it is certainly not pas-

sive. It is hard work both intellectually and spiritually. Yet
there is in it a certain deliberate surrender of control over
the way our mind usually works when we are thinking. It
starts with a kind of free association, but it goes beyond
that. It releases the so-called right hemisphere of the brain
that sees patterns and pictures where before we had seen
nothing but bits and pieces. Beyond that again I believe
that, sometimes at least, it offers us a glimpse of the glory of
the divine logic, the divine Logos.

Brainstorming

From this point on our discussion of how sermons grow
will be rooted in the specifics of one particular sermon on
Isaiah 41:5–10.

> 5 Coasts and islands saw it and were afraid,
>   the world trembled from end to end.
> 6   Each workman helps the others,
>   each man encourages his fellow.
> 7   The craftsman urges on the goldsmith,
>   the gilder urges the man who beats the anvil,
>   he declares the soldering to be sound;
>   he fastens the image with nails
>   so that it will not fall down.
>
> 8 But you, Israel my servant,
>   you, Jacob whom I have chosen,
>   race of Abraham my friend,
> 9   I have taken you up,
>   have fetched you from the ends of the earth,
>   and summoned you from its farthest corners,
>   I have called you my servant,
>   have chosen you and not cast you off:
> 10 fear nothing, for I am with you;
>   be not afraid, for I am your God.
>   I strengthen you, I help you,
>   I support you with my victorious right hand.

Let us assume that we have got started, have done the necessary exegetical work, have thought and prayed, and are ready to go.

We will have learned from our commentaries and from some of our translations that Isaiah 41:6–7 may properly belong between verses 20 and 21 of Isaiah 40. If this were accepted Isaiah 40:18–25 would be the appropriate pericope rather than Isaiah 41:5–10. But the case for transposition is not conclusive, and nothing substantial is at stake since in either position the same satirical contrast is being made between idolatry and true faith. Consequently the traditional reading of Isaiah 41:5–10 can be retained and the congregation saved an interesting but needless textual digression. More important, our reading of the passage will have shown, and our commentaries will have confirmed, that verses 5–7 are about the fears and frantic busyness of those who believe in gods who need to be supported (v. 7b); and verses 8–10 are about the security and serenity of those who believe in the true God, and who know that he supports them (v. 10b). The wider context of Isaiah 40:12–41:10 further confirms this identification of a theme that is distilled in Isaiah 41:10, "Fear nothing . . . I support you." "*I* support *you*," says God! The theme sentence is clear. "We don't support God, he supports us." The purpose statement paraphrases Isaiah 41:10. The sermon's purpose is to strengthen our assurance that, being supported by God, we need not be afraid. So much for systematic analysis. Sadly, the hardpressed pastor-preacher has little time for more if sufficient time is to be found to think. At this stage I let the mind wander free among the key affect and images of the material I am working with.

> *Isaiah 41:5–7 Fear* . . . worldwide . . . frantic busyness among the image-makers . . . mutual-admiration societies . . . activism and "works righteousness" . . . the church? . . . the gods who need to be nailed to their pedestals lest they fall . . . a blasphemous caricature of Christ, "the image of the invisible God," nailed to the cross?

Isaiah 41:8–10   Fearlessness . . . among God's true people
. . . the reason for assurance . . . servant, chosen, friend . . .
gathered . . . *ekklesia* . . . Israel, and the church as the new
Israel . . . relation of "I" and "you," God and us . . .
strengthen, help, support . . . *"I* support *you"* . . . we are supported, secure, safe, saved . . . fallen but no longer falling . . .
the fear of falling.

Let us leave all that amorphous stuff on one side for the
present and allow the mind to wander more widely in the
text of Scripture. Satirization of the idolaters was a favorite
prophetic sport in Old Testament times, Elijah setting the
pace and proving a tough act to follow (e.g., 1 Kings 18:27).
But what of the New Testament? One hardly needs the assistance of a wordbook or concordance to find oneself drawn
to Acts 17:22–31:

22   Then Paul stood up before the Court of Areopagus and
      said: 'Men of Athens, I see that in everything that concerns
23 religion you are uncommonly scrupulous. For as I was go-
      ing round looking at the objects of your worship, I noticed
      among other things an altar bearing the inscription "To an
      Unknown God". What you worship but do not know—this is
      what I now proclaim.
24   'The God who created the world and everything in it, and
      who is Lord of heaven and earth, does not live in shrines
25 made by men. It is not because he lacks anything that he
      accepts service at men's hands, for he is himself the univer-
26 sal giver of life and breath and all else. He created every
      race of men of one stock, to inhabit the whole earth's sur-
      face. He fixed the epochs of their history and the limits of
27 their territory. They were to seek God, and, it might be,
      touch and find him; though indeed he is not far from each
28 one of us, for in him we live and move, in him we exist; as
      some of your own poets have said, "We are also his off-
29 spring." As God's offspring, then, we ought not to suppose
      that the deity is like an image in gold or silver or stone,
30 shaped by human craftsmanship and design. As for the
      times of ignorance, God has overlooked them; but now he

31 commands mankind, all men everywhere, to repent, because he has fixed the day on which he will have the world
judged, and justly judged, by a man of his choosing; of this
he has given assurance to all by raising him from the dead.'

The parallels with Isaiah 40:12–41:10 are quite star-
tling. The theme is the same—idolatry; the style is the
same—satirical ("Men of Athens, I see that in everything
that concerns religion you are uncommonly scrupulous . . .");
even the poetry of the language is the same as it celebrates
the sovereignty and transcendence of God, yet his care for
his people and closeness to them. Admittedly, polemical satire against idolatry was common in Jewish tradition. But
Paul must have known Isaiah 40–41 from memory. Maybe
his sermon at Athens consciously or unconsciously echoes
the prophet's words. Certainly Acts 17:22–31 offers a suggestive New Testament counterpoint to Isaiah 40:12–41:10.
(Two Scripture readings, one Old Testament and the other
New, are the norm in some traditions including my own, so
the quest for an appropriate New Testament lesson when
preaching from the Old Testament can be a matter of consid-
erable importance.) But Paul does more than echo the
prophet's words. The christological and eschatological
thrust of Acts 17:30–31 is the climax of Paul's sermon and
points to a world the prophet dreamed of but never knew.
Note also that Paul speaks of a God who, though he does not
need our help, accepts it and accepts us as his children
(vv. 28–29).

We now have a messy pile of material before us drawn
from three sources: exegesis of a primary text; free association within the primary text; free association from the primary text to a secondary text. At this stage the sermon is a
good representation of chaos! It is "without form and void,
with darkness over the face of the abyss" (Gen. 1:2)—and no
doubt over the face of the struggling would-be preacher.
We cannot yet see the forest for the trees. This is where
thinking-praying begins in earnest. It is also the creative

stage at which sermons are conceived. The Spirit moves, and God says, "Let there be light" and there is light. Guided by such light as he has given us, let us see what order can come out of the chaotic material that now confronts us. There is living matter in that chaos if only we can discover its appropriate organic structure.

Organizing

Let us see now how this material might look once we discover its appropriate homiletic shape. It will need a strong conceptual skeleton, a healthy cardiovascular system of affect and image, a little fleshing out, and some muscle (see pp. 57–68). Above all, this complex material will require a vigorous organic unity that clearly embodies the theme sentence "We don't support God, he supports us." The organization of the material might follow a pattern something like this.

Introduction

Text: Isaiah 41:10. "I support you." Text storied in context. We don't support God. He supports us. Get this wrong and you get everything wrong. Like the idol worshipers, propping up their gods lest they tumble.

1. Sometimes we think we are supporting things and people when they are really supporting us.
   a. Experience as a football supporter finding oneself exhilarated, uplifted, supported by the team we were supporting. Trivial. But true also of more important things. Supporters find themselves supported.
   b. Moral values. One way of looking at: they need our support badly. But another way of looking at: we need their support even more. If right is no more than what I approve of and wrong no more than

what I dislike then the bottom drops out of life. It has no meaning. We need to be supported by the values we support, and we *are* so supported.

c. We support God! And he wants that support and uses it. But there is something comically wrong as soon as we start thinking of the church as God's supporters' club. Reread Isaiah 41:5–7 and let us get the feel of the sharp edge of the prophetic satire as it speaks to *our* idolatries, fears, and busyness. Reread Isaiah 41:8–10, "But you, Israel . . . fear nothing . . . *I* support *you.*" Feel the assurance of faith.

d. Harpo Marx leaning against the corner of a large bank, asked by a policeman if he thinks he is "propping up the bank or something," smiles and nods, is told to move on, moves on, and the bank collapses! Personal experience as pastor ill in hospital worried less that my church collapse than worried because it didn't. "What do we think we are doing here, propping up God or something?" If he had to, God could manage without us!

2. True, but not the whole truth.

a. God doesn't need our support but he wants it and uses it in ways beyond our imagining. "It is not because he lacks anything that he accepts 'the service of our hands'" (Acts 17:25). Why then? Because we are his children (Acts 17:29).

b. Remember how it was when the children were very small—or how it was when *we* were very small children. Children want to "help" Mum and Dad. The parents know the consequences may be dire. But this is how children learn to grow up. So they say, "All right, kids, let's do it together"—and in the end the job gets done. God says the same thing to us, little children in his family, and, however much we botch the job, in the end his will is done. God doesn't need us and the mess we make of his world, but he can use us in ways beyond our imagining.

c. Christ didn't need these nails—the true "image of the invisible God," nailed, flesh to wood, like some blasphemous caricature of what the ancient image-makers did. But he can use even that, supremely he can use that to say, "I support you, I can bear any-thing for you, even the sins of the world." Therefore, God "commands mankind, all men everywhere, to repent . . ." (Acts 17:30–31).

Conclusion

The primitive fear of falling. All supports gone. The nightmare of falling—many of us have dreamed it, some have lived it, some are living it now. The times when the bottom drops out of your world—bereavement, sickness, estrangement, unemployment, etc. And *all* of us share the nightmare, for we are all fallen people. But no longer falling. For in that fall *we are supported,* embraced, held, safe, saved, by arms outstretched on a cross. "Of this [God] has given assurance to all by raising [Christ] from the dead" (Acts 17:31). "Fear nothing . . . I support you with my victorious right hand" (Isa. 41:10).

Strategies of Development

The sermon just outlined is in no way offered as a "model." I chose this material simply because it usefully il-lustrates a number of strategies of development, some of which can be employed in most sermons. All of these devel-opments derive from the theme statement. But they are not merely repetitions of the theme; rather they are explora-tions of it in different dimensions, cognitive, affective, and volitional. The theme is "We don't support God, he supports us." Let me identify some of the strategies of develop-ment employed.

We think the theme. The doctrinal heart of the sermon is found in the interplay between the sovereignty and fatherhood of God. Ethical implications are suggested by "we are supported by the values we support." The psychological resonances of the theme are explored in "the fear of falling," etc.

We feel the theme. How it feels to be supported—secure, safe, saved. How it feels to lack support—insecure, afraid, lost. Notice that the words *falling, saved,* and *lost* are all emotive words carrying heavy theological freight. Comic and tragic dimensions of the theme are explored.

We activate the theme. The imperative, explicit in the text (which is repeated several times in different contexts) is implicit throughout the sermon—"fear nothing . . . I support you."

We invert the theme. (This and the following strategy are borrowed from procedures of musical composition.) The inversion of "we are supported" is "we are falling." The theme sentence itself is an explicit inversion—"We don't support God, he supports us." Whatever we are preaching about we should turn it upside down and see what it looks like from there.

We augment and diminish the theme. For the musician this means doubling or halving the length of the notes. For the preacher it means changing scale—from personal to societal to global to cosmic. (The theme does not become any more or less important by being augmented or diminished.) *This* sermon works mostly at the personal and societal levels. But the trivia of the ball game, Harpo Marx, and "let's do it together, kids" is a diminution from the personal, and the final image of the fall and the cross is an augmentation from the societal to the global and cosmic.

We picture and story the theme. All the imagery is clus-
tered round the polarity between support and falling,
security and fear. These images recur throughout the
sermon and are common to all of its storying. (Clusters
of related images work better than a variety of un-
related images.) Storying includes the narrative introduction which sets the text in context, the ball
game with its associated "church as God's supporters'
club," Harpo Marx, my personal discovery as a pastor
of my dispensability, "children helping," the glimpse
of the Passion story, the story of the nightmare of falling that ends in the security of Christ's embrace. All of
that material is a fusion of picture and story, part of
the cardiovascular system of the sermon.

Not all of these strategies of development will be equally
important in every sermon, but I find that they make a useful checklist. Have I thought, felt, and activated the theme?
Have I inverted, augmented, and diminished the theme?
Have I pictured and storied the theme? And if not, why
not? I believe that by the use of strategies such as these
healthy growth can be promoted within the organic unity
of a sermon.

7

Language and Delivery

Choosing the Words

Preaching is an oral, aural event. What is received by the congregation will be spoken words heard, not written words read. The way in which we use language when we address the ear is radically different from the way we use it when we address the eye. Words that speak well are often unreadable, as any verbatim transcription of a good discussion will soon show. But words that read well are often unspeakable! That is why even good sermonic essays are often, literally, unspeakable sermons.

We must learn to recover our natural oral, aural speech patterns. Most of our education, from junior high to postgraduate school, has conditioned us into believing that if we have anything really important to say, we should write it down. Consequently, literacy is rewarded and illiteracy is penalized. This is all very necessary for, even in graduate school, standards of literacy sometimes leave much to be desired. But our healthy ambition as students to improve our writing skills can easily inhibit our natural oral skills.

The meaning of words when written depends on careful

sentence construction, accurate punctuation, and so on. The meaning of words when spoken depends more on voice inflection than it does on sentence construction or punctuation. Notice how often a congregation reading a prayer aloud can ruin the sense and flow by well-intentioned pauses at all the commas. Notice also how difficult it is to speak a carefully wrought complex sentence. The eye can see in the construction of the sentence the relative importance and interplay of the various ideas it contains. But the ear is baffled when the sentence is read aloud. Take for instance the passage from the wordbook article quoted on page 62. It reads clearly, and says what it has to say with economy and precision. But if you read that passage aloud to a fellow student who cannot see the written text, you will soon find yourself in trouble. The reader may be enlightened but the listener will be lost. The same passage could be rewritten in a series of short simple sentences. The eye would now be baffled because it can no longer see how this sentence relates to that, and what is the relative importance of each. But the ear will be delighted if the short, multiple sentences are so framed and so inflected by the speaker that the listener can hear their interrelatedness and relative importance.

Sound, not syntax, determines what best makes sense to the ear. In sermon preparation let nothing go on paper that has not been adjudicated by the ear. Say everything aloud in a half a dozen different ways until what you are saying feels right to the tongue and sounds right to the ear. It does not matter what it looks like. It may not even make a sentence. All that matters is that it makes sense to the ear.

The reason that fully-scripted sermons sometimes fall flat is not primarily because the preacher is using a manuscript; rather it is because the style of the manuscript is literary, not oral. It reflects how the preacher usually writes but it bears no relationship to the way he or she usually talks. But there are other problems, too. A fully-scripted sermon involves some loss of eye contact. This can be minimized by keeping the manuscript high on the lectern so that eye movement alone can encompass both the manuscript and the congregation, the head held steady and not pecking at the paper. Pages written on one side only can be unobtrusively handled in a way that does not require a white flag of surrender to be waved every time a page is turned. The preacher can learn to keep the eye running well ahead of the tongue so that it is possible to phrase intelligently what has been written. All these tricks of the trade are not too hard to learn. The really difficult thing is to learn how to get on paper the kind of English we use naturally when we are speaking to a friend about something that is really important to us. Blessed are those so gifted, for they can script in full. The barrier that a manuscript can create has been greatly reduced because the manuscript is oral in style, not literary. It sounds right and real, yet it has precision and economy that the less fully scripted preacher seldom attains. Some of the greatest preachers I know script their sermons fully, and nobody knows or cares because of the skill with which they get themselves on to paper and off it again.

In my own early ministry I scripted my sermons in full. It was a valuable discipline. Later, as the demands made on me both as a pastor and as a preacher increased, I could no longer do so. I found it difficult and time-consuming to get on paper the way I naturally talk. (I am much more at ease as a speaker than as a writer.) So, under pressure of time rather than for any exalted theological or homiletic reasons, I had to change course. I had to invest most of my time in knowing exactly what I was going to say; but precisely how I was going to say it would have to wait until, within the context of worship, I faced my congregation. The result was undoubtedly a loss in economy and precision of expression, but the trade-off in terms of immediacy and spontaneity more than compensated for the loss.

Some of us, gifted by God with a natural fluency, do well to remember that the capacity to keep talking for twenty minutes or so does not necessarily mean that we are actually saying anything. Often, more hard thinking *and* more scripting is the appropriate prescription. But some of us, including some of the ablest pastors and students I have taught, have a latent gift for extempore speech that needs to be released and used. I know it can feel like a kind of arrogance to mount the pulpit steps as heralds of God's Word without knowing exactly what words we are going to use. But if we know exactly what we are going to say, the best way of saying it is sometimes best discovered not in the study, but in the pulpit when the thing the Spirit has conceived in us comes to its moment of delivery.

Let me suggest a compromise strategy between full scripting and briefly outlining. The procedure is especially useful for students beginning the study of homiletics but may also be used by experienced pastors who want to explore their latent gifts for extempore speech. Script the sermon in full, but make sure that every paragraph begins with a key sentence that distills the essence of that paragraph. Work hard on these key sentences to make them crisp and precise. Highlight all key sentences and important words and images with a yellow felt-tip pen. Let each key sentence be so constructed that it not only encapsulates the paragraph it introduces but also makes a smooth transition out of the key sentence of the previous paragraph. (If this proves impossible, there is probably a flaw in the sermon's structure.) When the time comes to deliver the sermon, start each paragraph with your carefully prepared sentence. Then, free of script, unpack the content of that sentence, allowing for an occasional glance to remind you of key words and images. When you are ready to close out the paragraph, *repeat the key sentence,* secure in the knowledge that it will not only accurately summarize what you have just said, but will provide a smooth transition into the next paragraph. This procedure sounds as if it might inhibit spontaneity. In practice it promotes it. It provides us with the safety net of a full script, yet the freedom to depart from it without fear of getting lost. The repetition of the appropriate key sentence will be welcomed by the ear and will immediately bring us back on course. In time the preacher may decide that the safety net can be left at home in the study; only the key sentences, words, and images will accompany him into the pulpit. From here it is a short step to dispensing with the full script altogether and concentrating on the sermon brief or outline. The time saved in writing can now be reinvested in thinking one's way through the sermon from beginning to end again and again. I find it helps to think aloud. I never "rehearse" sermons, but I talk to myself a lot!

We now have four procedures to choose from:

1. We can script in full in spoken English and learn how to use the script effectively.
2. We can script in full, highlighting key sentences, transitions, images, and words and using only the highlighted material most of the time but falling back on the full script whenever necessary.
3. We can script in full but take into the pulpit only the highlights in the form of a sermon brief.
4. We can dispense altogether with full script and go straight for the sermon brief, using time saved in writing for thinking and praying.

My own procedure is the last of these four. I find now that a full script obstructs me. I try to remember what I have written instead of investing all my resources in trying to say what I want to say. But that is a purely personal idiosyncracy. Any one of these four procedures is equally valid and can produce preaching of real splendor.

It is important to recognize that all that has been said in the last two chapters, on "Organic Unity" and "How Sermons Grow," is equally relevant whichever of these four procedures is adopted. Thinking-praying, brainstorming, organizing, and developing are part of the package for all of us. Until we have reached the stage where our material is at least organized and the sermon outlined, we are in no posi-

tion to begin a final draft of anything. We cannot know how
the sermon should begin until we know how it should end.
But to do that we must be able to see the sermon as a unitary
whole. At any point in the sermon we must know not just
where we have come from but where we are going. Never
waste precious time writing an elegant introduction to a
nonexistent theme. Prepare the introduction last.

T. S. Eliot was not thinking about sermons, but might
well have been when he wrote in *East Coker:*

> In my beginning is my end . . .
> What we call the beginning is often the end,
> And to make an end is to make a beginning . . .
> We shall not cease from exploration
> And the end of our exploring will be to arrive where we
>   started
> And know the place for the first time.

This is not only fine poetry, it also happens to be first-class
homiletic advice. It is good for a sermon to end where it began. It is often a sign of vigorous organic unity. The body of
the sermon is the exploration of the theme and "the end of
our exploring will be to arrive where we started and know
the place for the first time.'"

At the Time of Delivery

The great moment has come! The thing miraculously conceived in us is about to be delivered. Like prudent expectant
parents, we might as well make a checklist of the things
that have to be done—including some mundane trivia that
are easily forgotten in the excitement.

Before the Service

Allow a full hour (if possible immediately before the service and on the church premises) to think and pray your way
several times through the service as a whole and the sermon

in particular. If there is more than one service, try to get at least some quiet time between.

If you are not familiar with the building, check the public-address system, pulpit, and lectern before the congregation begins to arrive. Make sure your notes will stay put where you want them and do not keep slipping down to the bottom of the lectern, dragging your head with them. Try out the public-address system and test its tolerance to both the maximum and the minimum level of voice you want to use. Assess how far and in what directions its field of sensitivity extends.

Before the Sermon

Remember that the sermon is a part of worship. Worship is not just the warm-up for the great moment when we start to pontificate. Whether or not you are worship leader as well as preacher, share fully in what is happening. (If you are the worship leader, be sure you have prepared the whole of the service as carefully as you have the sermon.)

In the two or three minutes immediately before the sermon begins, go to your private prayers and focus your mind firmly on the task ahead. Relax the muscles of the upper body, shoulders, arms, neck, and face. (You will probably find they are tight as a bowstring.) Breath deeply and easily through the nose. (Your throat is probably dry and this will help.) Let the relaxation and deep breathing be the physical expression of your prayer.

The Reading of Scripture

Wherever possible, do it yourself immediately before the sermon. The reading of Scripture should be a great high point in the service. (What the Bible has to say for itself is far more important than anything we have to say about it.) I do not rehearse my sermons but I carefully rehearse every word of the Scripture that I shall read. All I have learned in my exegetical work goes into that reading. A word wrongly stressed or a sentence wrongly inflected can distort Scripture, and that is a serious matter. Good reading is a fruit of good exegesis. A brief introduction setting the passage in context and focusing on the central theme is often useful. Read narrative as if you had just been an eyewitness of the events recorded; read poetry as poetry and delight in its rhythms and parallelisms. Read familiar passages as if they had never been heard before. Reflect the mood of the passage—joy or grief, love or anger. Sometimes the Bible is read with a dreary homogenized pious propriety. The level of commitment to the reading of Scripture must be very high—not necessarily dramatic, but intense. Sometimes one hears preachers (who should know better) read Scripture as casually as they might a telephone book, then suddenly become animated and intense as soon as they begin the first sentence of their own sermon. That is as good as saying, "So much for the Word of God. Now let's get down to real business!" Usually we should start our sermon at a lower level of intensity than the level at which we have read Scripture.

Sermon Delivery

Be yourself. We are not professional actors playing the part of a preacher—perhaps even consciously impersonating our own favorite role model. The actor can be many characters, saint or sinner, genius or fool, hero or villain. We can only be ourselves. We have much to learn from the theater but we are amateurs in this field. Amateur theatricals are embarrassing in the pulpit. Yet preaching is a kind of dramatic presentation. Christian doctrine from creation to parousia is *the* cosmic drama whose script is Scripture. The crucified Carpenter who made the galaxies is the heart of the drama. His story in our stories, and ours in his, is the stuff of the drama (see chap. 2). If we are preaching the centralities of the Christian faith and really believe what we say, we cannot play it cool. There should be no need to superimpose phony histrionics or inauthentic emotionalism on what we are saying. But there is an urgent need on the part of many of us to recover our sense of the drama of the gospel, to feel it ourselves, and not to be afraid to let others see how we feel. Often we inhibit our authentic emotions in the pulpit and substitute for them inauthentic emotionalism which, even when it succeeds, can be dangerous and manipulative. The way in which the sense of drama is communicated will be determined by the temperament of the preacher. Some of us are naturally extrovert in speech and in body language, and what we are feeling is easily apparent. Some of us are more reticent in the display of our feelings, but we can eloquently convey through quiet intensity the degree of our emotional commitment. If we are really thinking and feeling what we are saying and allow that to be heard and seen as it is embodied in who we are, we will communicate effectively, and many of the technical problems of sermon delivery will take care of themselves.

Trust your reflexes. Allow yourself to do in the pulpit what you find yourself doing naturally when you are talking to a friend about something that really matters to you. Recognize the wide variety of pace, pitch, and volume that is part of the natural speech pattern of most of us. Notice how the color of the human voice changes as facial expression changes. Remember that it is not just the face but the whole body that wants to reflect what we are thinking and feeling, if only we will relax and trust our reflexes. Rehearsed gestures are usually as embarrassing as rehearsed smiles. But if we will relax the muscles of the whole upper body, we shall find that our face, hands, arms, and entire body are freed up. Our reflexes take over, our body language and gesture, and even the color of our voice, naturally mirror what we are saying.

Don't be afraid to pause. All of us, especially if we are not fully scripted, have a secret fear of getting stuck. Even the scripted preacher has a fear of losing the place or finding the last page of the manuscript has been left in the study. To reassure ourselves we keep talking . . . and talking . . . and talking. Silence is scary! It is interesting to see how, if for any reason a preacher does get stuck, even the semi-comotose congregation immediately sit up and take notice. They have been lulled to sleep by a steady flow of words but are stabbed awake by the silence. Take your time. Before you say anything, wait for the congregation to settle. After the reading of Scripture and before the sermon begins, allow time for the hearer to assimilate what has just been read and to adjust to the new relationship with you as you move from the words of Scripture to your own words.

Above all, remember that pause is the instrument through which we create verbal paragraphs. Paragraphs in written English are made by leaving some white space on the page, reinforced by a change of line. Paragraphs in spoken English are represented by a pause, often reinforced by a new vocal line—a change in pace, pitch, volume, or vocal color. Paragraphs, written or verbal, visible or aural, are essential to good communication. A book that goes on for many pages without a written paragraph to be seen is dreary to the eye. A sermon that goes on for many minutes without a verbal paragraph to be heard is dreary to the ear. The pause in the verbal paragraph fulfills a double function. It gives the hearer time to take aboard what has just been said, and it gives the speaker time to think ahead into the next paragraph and to move into the new material with some poise and assurance.

Sometimes we make unscheduled pauses as we search for a word, fail to find it, start the sentence over again, and this time say it better. Don't worry! The ear can usually distinguish clearly between the significant pause and the involuntary hesitation. Hesitation is no necessary obstacle to communication. It occurs constantly in ordinary intercourse and can actually become a part of the communication process. The mortal enemy of good communication is not the occasional hesitation but the relentless monotony of words without pause.

Use your voice. It doesn't need to be a great voice, nor does it need to be a very big one. A good public-address system (which no longer need cost the earth) makes clear diction more important for audibility than mere size of voice, and sensitivity of phrasing more important for intelligibility than mere quality of voice. Nevertheless, we must learn to use whatever instrument God has given us to its maximum potential.

Learn to breathe, not just for survival but for good voice production. Breathe from the diaphragm, not from the upper chest. When we have plenty of air in our lungs, meaning, not necessity, will determine where we should pause for breath and where we should not. Vary the length of phrases and notice how in speech, as in singing, the long phrase can be peculiarly eloquent, though it needs careful breath control. Vary phrase shapes. Not all sentences inflect downward as they end. A downward inflection signifies that the sentence is finishing as expected. An upward inflection signifies the unexpected. Where every sentence inflects downward, the sermon will sound predictable and monotonous, even when what is actually said is fresh and interesting.

Slovenly speech is unacceptable in the pulpit, so be prepared to make the lips, teeth, and tongue really work hard. That is what gives intensity to the spoken word, especially words quietly spoken. Remember that the voice is not produced in the throat. Think the sound forward to where the lips, teeth, and tongue are working. Explore the full range of your voice in pitch, in pace, and in volume, and do not be afraid to use the whole range available to you. In ordinary animated conversation, we often use a far wider range than we do in the pulpit. Once again the aim is to free us up to do in the pulpit what we do naturally elsewhere, to enable us to be ourselves—only more so!

8

Biblical Truth and Biblical Preaching

There is a famous sentence written by the sixteenth-century philosopher Francis Bacon in *An Essay on Truth*. Commenting on the confrontation between Christ and Pilate recorded in John 18:33–38 Bacon writes, " 'What is truth?' said jesting Pilate, and would not stay for an answer." I think Bacon got it wrong. Pilate may have been a lot of things—world-weary, impatient, contemptuous, scared— but on this occasion he was in no mood for jokes. Probably he was just plain confused. He could not understand what the young Galilean was talking about. Pilate wanted to talk about treason—"Are you the King of the Jews?" Jesus wanted to talk about truth—" 'King' is your word. My task is to bear witness to the truth."

When Pilate responds, "What is truth?" his question dramatizes not just the unforgettable moment of confrontation between a Roman governor and his Jewish prisoner, but a confrontation of two great cultures. Pilate represents the culture of the western world with its intellectual roots in Greece and its pragmatic roots in Rome. Jesus represents the culture of the people of the Book, a culture rooted wholly in the Book—in the Old Testament Scriptures. Truth for Pilate meant one thing, for Jesus it meant something different. (Scholars warn that the difference can be exaggerated but all agree the difference is real.) We like Pilate are children of a western culture but we also claim to be people of the Book. Sadly, when we speak of truth, not least in preaching, we often do so on Pilate's terms, not on Christ's.

For Pilate, whatever else truth was or was not, it was something you *thought*. "All human beings are mortal, Socrates is a human being, therefore Socrates is mortal"—Aristotle had taught him that. "The interior angles of a triangle are together equal to two right angles"—Euclid had taught him that. "A body displaces its own weight in any liquid in which it floats"—Archimedes had taught him that. Truth for Pilate, as it still is for us, was a function of the intellect; it was a proposition, a concept, a calculation. For Jesus, and for the people of the Book, truth was a much bigger thing. He and they had not been brought up on Aristotle or Euclid or Archimedes but on the Law and the Prophets and the Psalms. And that meant that for them truth was not just something you thought, it was something you also felt and did. Supremely, it was something Christ *was*.

If we are to understand the truth of our biblical faith and faithfully preach it, we must also understand the truth about truth. Truth in the biblical sense of the word is not merely, or even primarily, a child of the intellect. The Bible does not separate the intellect from the emotions and the will in the way that Pilate did and that we still do. In the Bible, truth is a function not just of propositions but of persons—supremely of the person of God. He is the truth, and we who have heard his voice are "of the truth," have become (however imperfectly) a part of the truth. As we "grow in Christ" we "bear witness to the truth," not just by what we say but by what we feel and by what we do—for that is what we truly *are*. "To this end *we* were born"—and reborn—"to bear witness to the truth," a truth that is not only thought, but also felt and done (see John 18:37).

Inevitably, as children of our western culture, we think of truth (whether we know it or not) in terms of our Greek philosophical heritage. We think of ourselves, as the Greeks did, as being constructed in a tripartite model. We have an intellect to think with, emotions to feel with, and a will to act with. But the intellect is meant to be king. It should control the emotions and instruct the will. Truth is regarded as a function of the intellect, and, in our western way of thinking, finds its appropriate expression in propositions, concepts, and calculations. Our western culture finds it difficult to understand any other kind of truth expressed in any other kind of way.

But truth in the biblical sense of the word *is* another kind of truth, and *does* express itself in another kind of way. It is expressed not only in propositions but also in people—supremely in the person of God. The Hebrew word for truth is *emeth*. The root meaning is "trustworthy," "faithful," "reliable." That personal meaning still survives in modern English usage where we talk, for instance, of "a true friend" or of people being "true to one another." That kind of truth is personal, not merely propositional. I *feel* you are my friend, and do not merely think so. And, if I am true to someone, that is not primarily a description of what I think but of what I feel and *do*. *Emeth* truth is like that. It is descriptive of persons not just of propositions and it is not only thought but also felt and done.

The New Testament word for truth is the Greek word *aletheia,* and precisely because it is a Greek word it carries with it overtones of Greek classical usage in which truth is seen as a child of the intellect and a function of proposition. But the Septuagint, the Greek translation of the Old Testament (which was the regular "pew Bible" in New Testament times), had translated the Hebrew *emeth* into the Greek *aletheia.* So throughout the New Testament we find a subtle blend of Hebraic and Greek thought forms. Nevertheless the Old Testament *emeth* meaning is seldom wholly muted. That is why John's Gospel can quite naturally talk about "doing the truth" (see John 3:21) and about "Jesus being the truth" (see John 14:6).

All this is more than a matter of academic interest. It goes to the heart of our understanding of the nature of the biblical truth we are commissioned to preach. Too easily we have allowed ourselves to be locked into the assumptions of our own western culture and have been content to preach Pilate's truth alone, the child of the intellect that expresses itself in propositions. We have tended to accept without question the tripartite division of human nature into intellect, emotion, and will. To do so is profoundly unbiblical. Neither the Old Testament nor the New recognizes any such division.

This is a matter of such critical importance to the preacher, and is so often overlooked, that I must allow myself one further step to clinch the argument before returning to our practical homiletic concerns. In biblical usage "the heart" (Old Testament *leb*, New Testament *kardia*) is not simply the seat of emotions. When the Bible wants to refer to that, it very accurately speaks of the "guts" (Old Testament *me'im*, New Testament *splagchna*, KJV, "bowels"). I do not simply feel with my heart, I think with it as well. Indeed, *leb* and *kardia* are frequently translated "mind" rather than "heart." The words do double duty according to context. In the same way the other Hebrew words translated "mind" in the Old Testament *(nephesh, ruach)* are feeling words as well as thinking words, and the New Testament counterparts *(dianoia, nous)* frequently carry overtones of that Old Testament usage. The hard line we draw between thinking and feeling, head and heart, is simply not there in the Bible.

So what about the will? Significantly, Hebrew has no separate word for it! I do not only think and feel with my heart, I will with it as well. In other words, the Bible knows nothing of that tripartite division of human nature into intellect, emotion, and will, and has little interest in a truth that is a child of the intellect alone. It speaks of a different kind of truth that is not just thought but also felt and done.

Many of our western theological and preaching traditions (including my own Scots Presbyterian tradition) have
been partial in their witness to biblical truth because they
have presented it in exclusively conceptional propositional
terms. The assumption has been that if people can be made
to think the right things then feeling and doing the right
things will naturally follow. Sadly, it does not. I am proud of
my own tradition, of its commitment to rigorous intellectual discipline, and of its deep concern for sound doctrine. I
know that if we think the wrong thing about God it will not
be long before we start feeling and doing the wrong thing as
well. Propositional truth matters. *Propositional truth about
God matters supremely.* But sound doctrine and propositional truth are not enough if the heart is unmoved and the
will remains irresolute. Felt truths are not to be despised.
Some people feel the truth of their faith with a profundity
that makes mere intellectual assent to the creeds and confessions look almost superficial by comparison. "Everyone
who *loves* . . . knows God" (1 John 4:7), no matter how inept
such lovers may sometimes be at expressing their love in
propositional orthodoxy. "The unloving know nothing of
God" (1 John 4:8), no matter how immaculate their intellectual orthodoxy may be. In the same way, some people "do the
truth" of their faith (see John 3:21) in a way that shames
both our intellectual orthodoxies and our felt traditional
pietisms. "Not everyone who calls me 'Lord, Lord' will
enter the kingdom of Heaven, but only those who do the will
of my heavenly Father" (Matt. 7:21). *The truth we preach
must be a truth not just thought, but also felt and done.*

Other traditions in the church have reacted sharply in
their preaching and worship against the kind of intellectu-
alism or quasi-intellectualism I have been describing. They
have rediscovered and celebrated the importance of felt
truth. They have recognized that what we feel (not least
about God and one another) is sometimes more important
than what we think, for what we think is sometimes no

more than a rationalization of what we already feel. But that healthy reaction against an excessive concern for propositional precision has sometimes led to theological irresponsibility and to self-indulgent emotionalism in preaching as in worship. Felt truths are not to be despised, but felt truth is not enough, unless it is reinforced by rigorous thinking and validated in Christian action. Our faith is not even a halfhearted faith if we only feel with our hearts, and do not think and act with them as well. *The truth we preach must be a truth not just felt, but also thought and done.*

Yet other preaching traditions, impatient with both propositional theology and emotional pietism, go straight for the truth done. Doing the truth becomes the heart of the gospel. Doctrine is muted and emotion is sometimes suspect. Personal lifestyle or social action or both become the principal instruments of Christian witness. There is great power in that witness and much to be learned from those who make it central. "You will recognize them by the fruits they bear" (Matt. 7:16). But "truth done" that is not part of a truth thought and felt can easily degenerate into a burdensome "works righteousness" and a new legalism. "What we ought to do" is made possible only by what God has done (see p. 22). Our response to God in love and gratitude for what he has done enables us to do what we ought to do, and that response is not merely ethical but intellectual and emotional. The truth done is a fruit of the Christian faith. But the truth done is not enough unless it is reinforced by sound doctrine and empowered by authentic feeling. *The truth we preach must be a truth not just done, but also thought and felt.*

The special kind of truth of which the Bible speaks is a holistic truth in which intellectual assent, emotional involvement, and volitional commitment are fused together when we wholeheartedly embrace the Christian faith. The faith we profess, the gospel we preach, is designed by God to soar on the thrust of these three engines, intellect, emotion, and will. All three are needed. A three-engine jet plane

can indeed fly on two engines, but it does not do so very
well. It can even keep airborne on one engine but that is
always dangerous. Some of our preaching tries to fly on one
engine—sometimes the intellect, sometimes the emotions,
sometimes the will, the choice depending on our tradition or
our temperament. More often we fly on two engines. Twin-
engine preaching is usually safe but seldom soars. Much
preaching in my own Calvinist tradition is twin-engine
preaching. It flies on the intellect and the will. It is concerned that people think the right thing and do the right
thing, and consequently it has tried to be doctrinally responsible and ethically concerned. But often such preaching can be emotionally uninvolved, and that leaves it less
than wholehearted and therefore less than biblical. We
must all make our own personal self-assessment. We must
identify the engine which for us is the weakest in its thrust,
and regularly service that engine with special care.

The whole of this book has been an attempt to describe a
theology and practice of preaching appropriate to the special kind of truth of which the Bible speaks. That is why in
chapter 1 we stressed that preaching is concerned not just
with telling people what to do but rather with "action enabled by insight, imperatives empowered by indicatives,
ethics rooted in theology, 'what we ought to do' made possible by what God has done" (see p. 22). That describes
a kind of preaching in which the thinking, feeling, and
doing elements of a sermon are all fused together in a
single thrust. In chapter 2 we saw how God reveals himself
to us in Scripture and in life, not in a series of systematic
theological propositions but rather in stories, his and ours.
Again, we can see that story is the most appropriate way
of conveying a truth that is not merely propositional but
holistic. In chapters 3 and 4 we looked in detail at the ways
in which we picture and story the conceptual doctrine
revealed to us throughout Scripture, employing exegetical
procedures appropriate to the special kind of truth Scripture contains. In chapter 5, speaking of the organic unity of

the sermon, we saw how a conceptual skeleton, an emotive cardiovascular system, and a volitional muscle are all interdependent parts of the body of a sermon—once again reflecting the fusion of thinking, feeling, and doing characteristic of biblical truth. In chapter 6 we tried to exemplify the same kind of truth embodied in procedures of sermon preparation as we thought the theme, felt the theme, and activated the theme. In chapter 7 we discussed how such truth could find oral expression through the appropriate choice of words and their effective delivery. Now at last in chapter 8 we have made explicit the hidden premise that has been implicit throughout. In preaching, the whole person is addressed by the whole truth. The gospel is most clearly heard when we speak wholeheartedly, heart to heart, with hearts that not only feel, but also think and act.

There is one final problem. I have described biblical truth as a truth not only thought but also felt and done. That is so. But in so describing it I have had to fall back on our western way of thinking of human nature in terms of intellect, emotion, and will. As we have seen, that is an unbiblical way of thinking. To think biblically we must discard that tripartite model and learn to think passionately and to feel thoughtfully, for only so can we act wholeheartedly. In our preaching as in our living, we have got to get together the truth that we think, the truth that we feel, and the truth that we do. This book has tried to suggest some ways in which we can facilitate that integration and fusion of thinking, feeling, and doing that biblical truth demands. But, in the end of the day, that fusion does not happen as a consequence of anything that *we* do. It is a gift of grace. In the Bible, grace and truth are natural allies and it is grace that enables us to get together truth thought with truth felt and truth done. At the time of a sermon's delivery, as at the time of its conception, there can come a miraculous moment when what we are thinking and feeling and saying are no longer three things but one. Then we know that we are near the Truth, and in that moment we experience grace. I wish I could be more precise, but I speak of a Truth that is the Word beyond words.

Nevertheless, although I cannot express in clear concepts what I have just been trying to say, I can tell you what it is like. It is not inappropriate that this book should end not with a concept but with a simile, not with a proposition but a picture, not with a summary but with a story.

When I was a boy of about fourteen I came reluctantly to the conclusion that I should have to learn to dance. I didn't like the idea, but I could see that my friends who were good dancers were enjoying certain social fringe benefits that I was missing. I decided that before making a public exhibition of my awkwardness I would master the art secretly and in private. I bought myself a book called *Teach Yourself to Dance*. It contained detailed instructions and elaborate diagrams showing exactly what to do and where to put your feet. (I'm talking of ballroom dancing 1930s style, not of today's discos!) I mastered these instructions and memorized the diagrams—I really knew the book. Intellectually I had mastered the subject matter. I also spent many hours trying to put what I knew into practice. I did so alone in my bedroom, using a pillow for a partner and studying my progress in the wardrobe mirror.

What I saw in the mirror was not reassuring! I was putting my feet in all the right places, for I knew the book, and I was doing what the book said. But something clearly was missing. I was thinking the right things and doing the right things, but I couldn't get the feel of it, and in consequence everything I did seemed clumsy—graceless.

Then one night at a party a nice girl who knew of my difficulty said, "Come on, try it with me." So I did, and to begin with I felt even more of a fool because I was so awkward and she was so full of grace. Then something strange happened. A little of her grace seemed to pass to me and I began to get the feel of it. For the first time all I had learned in the book began to make sense, and even the painful practice in front of the mirror began to pay off. What had been contrived now became natural, what had been difficult now became easy, what had been a burden now became a joy—because at last I had got together what I was thinking and what I was feeling and what I was doing. In that moment I experienced a kind of grace, and it was very beautiful.

We profess and preach another and much greater kind of grace. It comes to us when we get together truth thought, truth felt, and truth done. We've got to know the Book, that comes first. And we've got to do what the Book says, follow in Christ's steps. But we can know truth and even do it and still be awkward, inadequate, graceless, until we get the feel of it. That is when we need to remember that it is not meant to be a solo dance. Christ wants us, his church, his clumsy bride, to try it with him. To begin with, we often feel more inadequate than ever when we do that, because we are so awkward and he is so full of grace. Then it happens, in our preaching as in our Christian living. We share in his grace. All the Book says comes alive, and, when we preach it, what used to be contrived now becomes natural, what used to be a labor now become spontaneous, what used to be a burden now becomes a blessing, what used to be law now becomes gospel. Why? Because we are learning the meaning of grace; because now God's Truth, thought, felt, and done, is embracing us in the dance—the Truth that stood before Pilate but that Pilate never recognized, because Pilate thought truth was a proposition not a person, a diagram not a dancer.

There is a song of the 1960s by Sidney Carter about Christ, "The Lord of the Dance." The original goes back some four hundred years to a carol called "My Dancing Day." (The early carols were all music for dancing.) The words of both the old and the new version tell the whole story of Christ's birth, life, death, and resurrection. The old carol tells it in great detail and in many verses. Christ is the singer, and after each verse he repeats a tender refrain to us, his beloved:

> Sing, O my love, my love, my love,
> This have I done for my true love.

The modern refrain is more robust but no less appropriate:

> 'Dance then, wherever you may be,
> I am the Lord of the Dance,' said he,
> 'And I'll lead you all wherever you may be,
> I'll lead you all in the dance,' said he.

"And we beheld his glory, . . . full of grace and truth" (John 1:14, KJV). "The grace of our Lord Jesus Christ be with you all."

For Further Reading

Exegetical Tools

There are certain basic reference works which will be of great help to the preacher in approaching the biblical text. In addition to standard tools such as concordances, the following works will be found useful:

The *Eight Translation New Testament* (published by Tyndale) offers the chance for the preacher to see several versions of the text at a glance.

Commentaries which cover the whole of the Bible in a single volume are helpful in quickly giving the preacher exegetical insight without being overwhelming. *Peake's Commentary on the Bible* (edited by Matthew Black, Nelson, 1962) is older, but includes some of the finest British scholarship. The *Jerome Biblical Commentary* (edited by Raymond E. Brown et al., Prentice-Hall, 1968) is the product of Roman Catholic biblical scholarship, offering a frequently helpful perspective. Two good commentaries with a conservative approach are *The New Bible Commentary: Revised* (edited by Donald Guthrie et al., Eerdmans, 1970) and *The International Bible Commentary* (edited by F. F. Bruce, Zondervan, 1986).

Bible dictionaries and theological wordbooks are invaluable. The *New Bible Dictionary* (edited by J. D. Douglas et al., Tyndale, 1982) is an excellent tool, broad in it coverage and modest in its cost. Alan Richardson's *A Theological Word Book of the Bible* (Macmillan, 1950) has been a constant and faithful companion to me throughout my ministry. Colin Brown's *Dictionary of New Testament Theology* in three volumes (Zondervañ, 1975) is extensive in its scope without being inaccessible, offering helpful information on the Old Testament as well.

For guidance on the choice of individual commentaries a good place to start is with *Old Testament Books for Pastor and Teacher* by Brevard S. Childs (Westminster, 1977) and with its companion volume by Ralph P. Martin, *New Testament Books for Pastor and Teacher* (Westminster, 1984). Even bibliographies as recent as these, however, can miss some fine new commentaries.

A useful guide through the process of biblical exegesis is *How to Read the Bible for All It's Worth* by Gordon D. Fee and Douglas Stuart (Zondervan, 1982).

Preaching Perspectives

It is important to view the preaching task from a number of different vantage points. The following introductory works on preaching are especially recommended.

An Introduction to Contemporary Preaching by J. Daniel Baumann (Baker, 1972) is a thorough and helpful survey of the preaching process which offers special help in communication theory. *Preaching the Good News* by George E. Sweazey (Prentice-Hall, 1976) is a lively and encyclopedic introduction, a little weak perhaps on the biblical basis of preaching but still interesting. *Between Two Worlds* by John R. Stott (Eerdmans, 1982) is a first-rate statement about preaching from a biblical conservative who is very much in touch with the contemporary world. Fred Craddock's new textbook, simply called *Preaching*

(Abingdon, 1985), is a splendid piece of work from one of the most respected homileticians in America. A valuable survey of contemporary writing on the preaching task is found in Edward F. Markquart's *Quest for Better Preaching* (Augsburg, 1985). His book is filled with homiletic wisdom and quotations drawn from a variety of writers.

Sermon Triggers

Reading the sermons of other preachers is both helpful and dangerous. I have found myself stimulated by what I call "sermon triggers"—biblical and theological insights which help to spark sermons without threatening to give them actual shape. I enjoy Clyde S. Kilby's anthology of quotations drawn from the writings of C. S. Lewis, *A Mind Awake* (Harcourt Brace Jovanovich, 1968). The works of Frederick Buechner are consistently stimulating and provocative, especially *Wishful Thinking* (Harper and Row, 1973) and *Peculiar Treasures* (Harper and Row, 1979). His Lyman Beecher Lectures on Preaching, entitled *Telling the Truth* (Harper and Row, 1977), are excellent. More sermon triggers are to be found in books of quotations such as *Living Quotations for Christians,* edited by Sherwood E. Wirt and Kersten Beckstrom (Harper and Row, 1974).

Subject Index